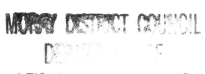

CONTENTS

EDITORIAL
Food Editor: Rachel Blackmore
Subeditor: Ella Martin
Editorial Assistant: Sheridan Packer
Editorial Coordinator: Margaret Kelly

DESIGN AND PRODUCTION
Manager: Sheridan Carter
Layout and Finished Art: Lulu Dougherty
Design: Frank Pithers

Published by J.B. Fairfax Press Pty Limited
80-82 McLachlan Avenue
Rushcutters Bay, NSW 2011, Australia
A.C.N. 003 738 430

Formatted by J.B. Fairfax Press Pty Limited
Printed by Toppan Printing Co, Singapore

JBFP 364
Indian Home Cooking
Includes Index
ISBN 1 86343 201 9

ABOUT THIS BOOK

THE PANTRY SHELF

Unless otherwise stated, the following ingredients used in this book are:

Cream — Double, suitable for whipping
Flour — White flour, plain or standard
Sugar — White sugar

In this book the recipes use fresh chillies, ginger and garlic. These ingredients, already minced in bottles, are available from supermarkets and will save you having to crush, chop and mince when time is short. Once opened they keep well in the refrigerator.

Remember when cooking Indian food much depends on your personal taste and that the quantities of spices can be varied to suit. Do not be put off making a recipe just because you do not have one of the ingredients – in most cases a spice can be omitted and while the flavour will be slightly different the result will still be delicious.

MICROWAVE OVEN

Where microwave instructions occur in this book a microwave oven with a 650 watt output has been used. Wattage on domestic microwave ovens varies between 500 and 700 watts. It may be necessary to vary the cooking times slightly depending on your oven.

WHAT'S IN A TABLESPOON?

NEW ZEALAND
1 tablespoon = 15 mL OR 3 teaspoons

UNITED KINGDOM
1 tablespoon = 15 mL OR 3 teaspoons

AUSTRALIA
1 tablespoon = 20 mL OR 4 teaspoons

The recipes in this book were tested in Australia where a 20 mL tablespoon is standard. All measures are level.

The tablespoon in the New Zealand and United Kingdom sets of measuring spoons is 15 mL. In many recipes this difference will not matter. For recipes using baking powder, gelatine, bicarbonate of soda, small quantities of flour and cornflour, simply add another teaspoon for each tablespoon specified.

HOT AND SPICY MEAL

Clockwise from right: Spicy Vegetables, Spinach Raitha, Cucumber Mint and Basil Salad, Spicy Red Prawns, Bombay Hot Lentils

INDIAN
Home Cooking

MEERA BLACKLEY
Photography MICHAEL COOK

J B F P

A J.B. Fairfax Press Publication

Spicy Red Prawns
Lal Jhinga

Spicy Vegetables
Pau Bahji

Red Chilli Chutney
Lal Mirch Chutney

Spinach Raitha
Palak Raitha

Bombay Hot Lentils
Bombay Mung Dhal

Cucumber, Mint
and Basil Salad
*Kakri, Phudina and
Tulsi Sambal*

Plates Joan Bowers

SPICY RED PRAWNS

Oven temperature
160°C, 325°F, Gas 3

16 large uncooked prawns, shelled
and deveined
3 large tomatoes, peeled, seeded
and chopped
1 tablespoon vegetable oil
1 small bunch coriander, leaves
removed and chopped

MARINADE
6 cloves garlic, finely chopped
2 teaspoons finely chopped fresh ginger
8 fresh red or green chillies,
finely chopped
3 tablespoons lemon juice
1 tablespoon caster sugar
salt

1   To make marinade, place garlic,
ginger, chillies, lemon juice, sugar and salt
to taste in a bowl and mix to combine.
Add prawns and toss to coat with
marinade. Cover and marinate in the
refrigerator for 15-20 hours.

2   Place tomatoes in a food processor or
blender and process until smooth.

3   Heat oil in a wok or large frying pan,
reduce heat to low, add prawns and
marinade and cook, stirring constantly,
for 2-3 minutes. Transfer prawns to a
casserole dish, add tomatoes and
coriander and mix well to combine.
Cover and bake for 30 minutes.

Serves 4

VARIATION

Oven temperature
180°C, 350°F, Gas 4

For a milder dish, reduce the
quantity of chillies and do not
marinate. If you wish to make
a hotter dish, add 2-4 extra
chillies.

Spicy Lamb or Veal: In place of the
prawns use 1 kg/2 lb diced lamb or veal.
Place meat in marinade and mix to
combine. Cover and refrigerate for
15-20 hours.
    Heat oil in a wok or large frying pan.
Add meat and marinade and cook,
stirring, for 2-3 minutes or until meat
changes colour. Reduce heat to low, cover
pan and cook, stirring occasionally, for 20
minutes or until meat is tender. Transfer

meat to a casserole dish, add tomatoes
and coriander and mix well to combine.
Cover and bake for 30 minutes.

To microwave: Place meat mixture,
tomatoes and coriander in a microwave-
safe casserole dish, cover and cook on
MEDIUM (70%) for 20 minutes or until
meat is tender.

Serves 6

*Spicy Red Prawns: (at back) prawns in marinade
and tomato mixture; (at front) pan-cooking prawns*

SPICY VEGETABLES

250 g/8 oz baby new potatoes, diced
1/2 small cauliflower, broken into florets
250 g/8 oz fresh or frozen peas
2 tablespoons vegetable oil
3 small onions, finely chopped
2 teaspoons finely chopped fresh ginger
4 cloves garlic, finely chopped
1 fresh red or green chilli,
finely chopped
1 teaspoon cumin seeds
salt
2 tomatoes, diced
1/4 cup/60 mL/2 fl oz lemon juice
1 bunch fresh coriander, leaves removed
and chopped
8 whole Pau (fried bread rolls,
see page 73)

DRY SPICE MIXTURE
1 teaspoon ground cumin
1 teaspoon ground coriander
1/2 teaspoon ground cinnamon
1/2 teaspoon ground turmeric
1/4 teaspoon ground fennel
1/4 teaspoon cayenne pepper
1/4 teaspoon mango powder
1/4 teaspoon ground bay leaves

1   Boil or microwave potatoes, cauliflower and peas, separately, until tender. Drain and set aside.

2   For spice mixture, place cumin, coriander, cinnamon, turmeric, fennel, cayenne pepper, mango powder and bay leaves in a bowl and mix to combine. Set aside.

3   Heat oil in a large heavy-based saucepan, add onions, ginger, garlic, chilli, cumin seeds and salt to taste and cook over a low heat, stirring occasionally, for 10-15 minutes or until onions are soft and transparent. Add tomatoes and cook, stirring occasionally, for 10 minutes or until tomatoes are soft and pulpy. Add spice mixture and simmer, stirring constantly, for 2 minutes. Add cooked vegetables and lemon juice and cook, stirring occasionally, for 5 minutes or until vegetables are heated through. Reduce heat to low, cover and simmer for 5 minutes longer. Just prior to serving, stir in chopped coriander. Serve with Pau.

To microwave: Microwave potatoes, cauliflower and peas, separately, until just tender. Set aside. Place oil, onions, ginger, garlic, chilli, cumin seeds and salt to taste in a microwave-safe dish and cook on HIGH (100%) for 10 minutes. Add tomatoes and cook on MEDIUM (70%) for 10 minutes longer. Stir in spice mixture and cook on LOW (30%) for 5 minutes. Add cooked vegetables and cook on HIGH (100%) for 10 minutes longer or until vegetables are heated through.

Serves 4

Plain bread can be served with this dish instead of the Pau if you wish.

Red Chilli Chutney

10-12 fresh red chillies
10-12 cloves garlic
pinch caster sugar (optional)
salt
water

Place chillies, garlic, sugar (if using) and salt to taste in a food processor or blender and process to chop. With machine running, add enough water to form a paste. Store in the refrigerator in an airtight container.

Makes 1 x 125 g/4 oz jar

When handling fresh chillies, do not put your hands near your eyes or allow them to touch your lips. To avoid discomfort and burning, you might like to wear rubber gloves.

Spinach Raitha

1 bunch/500 g/1 lb English spinach
1 cup/200 g/6$^{1}/_{2}$ oz natural yogurt
pinch salt
pinch freshly ground black pepper
pinch paprika
pinch mango powder
2 small fresh red or green chillies, chopped

1   Steam or microwave spinach until soft. Drain, squeezing to remove excess liquid. Place spinach in a food processor or blender and process to make a purée.

2   Place yogurt in a bowl and beat until smooth. Stir in salt, black pepper, paprika, mango powder, chillies and spinach and mix to combine.

Makes 1 cup/250 mL/8 fl oz

Natural yogurt and yogurt-based dishes are refreshing accompaniments to spicy food.

Red Chilli Chutney

Bowl Joan Bowers

9

BOMBAY HOT LENTILS

water
200 g/6$\frac{1}{2}$ oz mung dhal (small yellow lentils), cleaned and soaked
$\frac{1}{2}$ teaspoon ground turmeric
1 teaspoon finely chopped fresh ginger
1 tablespoon vegetable oil
salt
1 tablespoon tamarind
1 tablespoon brown sugar
$\frac{1}{2}$ bunch fresh coriander, leaves removed and chopped
3 tablespoons flaked coconut
2 teaspoons garam masala

WHOLE SPICE MIXTURE
90 g/3 oz ghee or butter
1 teaspoon cumin seeds
1 teaspoon black mustard seeds
$\frac{1}{4}$ teaspoon fenugreek seeds
2 tablespoons chopped curry leaves
3 fresh red or green chillies, finely chopped
2 teaspoons finely chopped fresh ginger

To prepare lentils for cooking, pick them over and remove any small sticks or stones, then place lentils in a large bowl. Fill bowl with water and stir, using your hands, until water is cloudy. Drain and repeat until the water is clear. You will probably need to repeat the procedure 3-4 times. Drain, pour over fresh water and set aside to soak for 45 minutes.

1   Place 2 cups/500 mL/16 fl oz water in a large saucepan and bring to the boil. Stir in lentils, turmeric, ginger, oil and salt to taste and cook over a low heat, stirring occasionally, for 30-45 minutes or until lentils are very soft. Remove pan from heat and mash lentil mixture.

2   Place tamarind in a small bowl, pour over 1 cup/250 mL/8 fl oz hot water and set aside to soak for 20 minutes. Drain liquid from tamarind mixture, then push tamarind pulp through a fine sieve and set aside. Reserve juice for another use.

3   For spice mixture, heat ghee or butter in a separate large saucepan, add cumin seeds, mustard seeds, fenugreek seeds, curry leaves, chillies, ginger and salt to taste and cook, stirring, for 1 minute. Add lentil mixture and 4 cups/1 litre/1$\frac{3}{4}$ pt water to spice mixture and bring to the boil. Stir reserved tamarind pulp and brown sugar into lentil mixture and cook, stirring occasionally, for 5 minutes longer.

4   Stir in fresh coriander, coconut and garam masala and cook for 2 minutes longer.

To microwave: Place lentils, turmeric, ginger and oil in a microwave-safe dish. Pour over 1$\frac{1}{2}$ cups/375 mL/12 fl oz boiling water, cover and cook on HIGH (100%) for 8 minutes, then reduce to MEDIUM (70%) and cook for 8 minutes longer. Add more water during cooking if lentils start to dry out. Mash lentils and set aside.

In a separate large microwave-safe dish, place ghee or butter, cumin seeds, mustard seeds, fenugreek seeds, curry leaves, chillies and ginger and cook on HIGH (100%) for 2 minutes. Add lentil mixture and 4 cups/1 litre/1$\frac{3}{4}$ pt boiling water and cook on MEDIUM (70%) for 8 minutes. Stir in reserved tamarind pulp and brown sugar and cook on LOW (30%) for 8 minutes. Stir in fresh coriander, coconut and garam masala and cook on LOW (30%) for 2 minutes longer. Season to taste with salt.

Serves 4

Bombay Hot Lentils: (at back) mashed lentil mixture; (at front) finished dish

CUCUMBER, MINT AND BASIL SALAD

1 cucumber, diced
$^1/_2$ bunch fresh mint, leaves removed
and chopped
$^1/_2$ bunch fresh basil, leaves removed
and chopped
2 small fresh red or green chillies,
finely chopped

LEMON AND SPICE DRESSING
2 teaspoons lemon juice
pinch mango powder
pinch paprika
pinch salt

1   Place cucumber, mint, basil and
chillies in a salad bowl.

2   To make dressing, place lemon juice,
mango powder, paprika and salt in a
screwtop jar and shake well to combine.
Pour dressing over salad and toss to
combine.

Serves 4

11

FAMILY MEAL

Clockwise from right: Spicy Tomato with Bread, Lettuce and Dill Salad, Chicken Coconut Curry, Plain White Rice, Plain Raitha

Chicken Coconut
Curry
Murgh Nariyal Curry

Plain White Rice
Sada Chawal

Mint and Tomato
Chutney
Phudina Tamatar Chutney

Peas and Potatoes
Mater Allo Bhaji

Cauliflower Kheema
Gobi Kheema

Spicy Tomato with
Bread
Tamatar Bhaji Pau

Lettuce and Dill Salad

Plain Raitha
Sada Raitha

CHICKEN COCONUT CURRY

This recipe can also be made using diced veal, lamb or beef in place of the chicken.

1 tablespoon vegetable oil
2 teaspoons cumin seeds
2 teaspoons finely chopped fresh ginger
2-3 fresh red or green chillies, finely chopped
4-5 cloves garlic, finely chopped
500 g/1 lb boneless chicken breast fillets, diced
1 teaspoon ground turmeric
1 teaspoon mango powder
1 teaspoon ground cumin
1 teaspoon ground coriander
$^{1}/_{2}$ teaspoon garam masala
pinch ground cloves
pinch ground cinnamon
pinch ground cardamom
1$^{3}/_{4}$ cups/440 mL/14 fl oz coconut milk
salt

1 Heat oil in a heavy-based saucepan over a low heat, add cumin seeds, ginger, chillies and garlic and cook, stirring, for 1 minute.

2 Add chicken, mix well, cover and cook, stirring occasionally, for 20 minutes or until chicken is tender.

3 Stir in turmeric, mango powder, ground cumin, coriander, garam masala, cloves, cinnamon and cardamom and cook, stirring, for 3-5 minutes. Add coconut milk, bring to simmering and season to taste with salt. Remove pan from heat and serve.

To microwave: Place oil, cumin seeds, ginger, chillies, garlic and chicken in a microwave-safe dish, cover and cook on HIGH (100%) for 4-5 minutes. Stir and cook on MEDIUM (70%) for 10 minutes longer.
   Stir in mango powder, ground cumin, coriander, garam masala, cloves, cinnamon and cardamom and cook on LOW (30%) for 5 minutes. Stir in coconut milk and cook on MEDIUM (70%) for 5 minutes longer. Season to taste with salt and serve.

Serves 6

Any leftover sauce is delicious mixed into cooked mixed vegetables. Boil, steam or microwave the required quantity of vegetables, drain and mix into sauce. Heat and serve with rice or toasted bread.

PLAIN WHITE RICE

Lemon juice makes the rice stay fresh longer, and the oil separates the grains and gives them a shiny appearance.

4 cups/1 litre/1$^{3}/_{4}$ pt water
2 cups/440 g/14 oz basmati rice, washed
1 teaspoon lemon juice
1 teaspoon vegetable oil
salt

Place water in a large heavy-based saucepan and bring to the boil. Stir in rice, lemon juice, oil and salt to taste, cover and simmer for 15 minutes or until rice is cooked.

To microwave: Place rice, lemon juice and oil in a large microwave-safe container, pour over boiling water, cover and cook on HIGH (100%) for 8 minutes, then on LOW (30%) for 10-12 minutes longer or until liquid is absorbed and rice is tender.

Serves 6

A little turmeric can be added to the rice before cooking to give a yellow-coloured rice with an aromatic flavour.

Mint and Tomato Chutney

4 large tomatoes, diced
1 bunch fresh mint, leaves removed and
coarsely chopped
$^1/_2$ cup/90 g/3 oz brown sugar
1 cinnamon stick
2 bay leaves
1 teaspoon mixed spice
2 teaspoons finely chopped fresh ginger
2 fresh red or green chillies, chopped
$^1/_4$ cup/60 mL/2 fl oz white wine vinegar

1   Place tomatoes, mint, sugar, cinnamon stick, bay leaves, mixed spice, ginger, chillies and vinegar in a heavy-based saucepan and cook over a low heat, stirring every 5 minutes, for 45 minutes or until mixture reduces and thickens.

2   Spoon chutney into a warm sterilised jar, cover and label when cold.

To microwave: Place tomatoes, mint, sugar, cinnamon stick, bay leaves, mixed spice, ginger, chillies and vinegar in a large microwave-safe container, cover and cook on HIGH (100%) for 15 minutes, stir and cook on MEDIUM (70%) for 15 minutes longer.

Mint and Tomato Chutney

Makes 1 x 125 g/4 oz jar

This chutney should be stored in the refrigerator and will keep for 4-6 weeks.
Use 440 g/14 oz canned tomatoes in place of the fresh tomatoes, if you wish.

Peas and Potatoes

1 tablespoon vegetable oil
2 teaspoons cumin seeds
2 teaspoons finely chopped fresh ginger
2 fresh red or green chillies,
finely chopped
4 potatoes, diced
salt
4 tomatoes, diced
250 g/8 oz fresh or frozen peas, boiled,
cooking water reserved
$^1/_2$ teaspoon mango powder
$^1/_2$ teaspoon ground turmeric
1 teaspoon ground cumin
1 teaspoon ground coriander
2 teaspoons chopped fresh coriander

1   Heat oil in a heavy-based saucepan over a low heat, add cumin seeds, ginger, chillies, potatoes and salt to taste and cook, stirring frequently, for 10-15 minutes or until potatoes are just tender.

2   Add tomatoes and cook for 5 minutes longer or until tomatoes are soft and pulpy. Stir in peas, $^3/_4$ cup/185 mL/6 fl oz reserved cooking water, mango powder, turmeric, ground cumin and ground coriander and mix well to combine. Cook over a low heat for 5 minutes longer. Just prior to serving, stir in fresh coriander.

To microwave: When cooking this dish in the microwave do not cook the peas first. Place oil, cumin seeds, ginger, chillies, potatoes, peas, and $^1/_4$ cup/ 60 mL/2 fl oz water in a microwave-safe container. Mix well to combine, cover and cook on HIGH (100%) for 10 minutes. Add tomatoes and cook on MEDIUM (70%) for 10 minutes. Stir in mango powder, turmeric, ground cumin and ground coriander and cook on LOW (30%) for 5 minutes. Just prior to serving, season to taste with salt and stir in fresh coriander.

Serves 6

For a change, you might like to use green beans in place of the peas in this recipe.

Cauliflower Kheema

1 tablespoon vegetable oil
2 teaspoons finely chopped fresh ginger
2 fresh red or green chillies,
finely chopped
2 teaspoons cumin seeds
2 bay leaves
salt
2 large onions
1 cauliflower, cut into small florets and
very finely chopped
$^1/_2$ cup/125 mL/4 fl oz water
4 large tomatoes, finely chopped
1 teaspoon ground coriander
1 teaspoon ground cumin
1 teaspoon garam masala
1 teaspoon mango powder
$^1/_2$ teaspoon ground turmeric

Serves 6

1   Heat oil in a heavy-based saucepan over a low heat. Add ginger, chillies, cumin seeds, bay leaves and salt to taste and cook, stirring, for 1 minute.

2   Place onions in a food processor or blender and process until almost puréed. Add onions to pan and cook, stirring frequently, for 12-15 minutes or until onions are golden. Add cauliflower and water and cook, stirring, for 5-6 minutes or until cauliflower is tender.

3   Add tomatoes and cook, stirring occasionally, for 10 minutes. Stir in coriander, ground cumin, garam masala, mango powder and turmeric and cook for 5 minutes longer.

Butternut pumpkin is also delicious cooked in this way.

Peas and Potatoes,
Cauliflower Kheema

SPICY TOMATO WITH BREAD

2 tablespoons oil
2 large onions, chopped
1 teaspoon cumin seeds
2 teaspoons finely chopped fresh ginger
2 fresh red or green chillies, chopped
salt
6 large tomatoes, peeled and chopped
1 teaspoon ground cumin
1 teaspoon ground coriander
$^1/_2$ teaspoon mango powder
$^1/_4$ teaspoon ground turmeric
2 bunches fresh coriander, leaves
removed and finely chopped
8 whole Pau (fried bread rolls,
see page 73)

1   Heat oil in a heavy-based saucepan, add onions, cumin seeds, ginger, chillies and salt to taste. Cook, stirring frequently, for 10 minutes or until onions are a light golden colour.

2   Stir in tomatoes and cook for 5-7 minutes. Stir in ground cumin, ground coriander, mango powder, turmeric and fresh coriander and cook for 2 minutes longer. Serve with Pau.

To microwave: Place oil, onions, cumin seeds, ginger and chillies in a microwave-safe container and cook, uncovered, on HIGH (100%), stirring every 5 minutes, for 15 minutes or until onions are a light golden colour and soft. Add tomatoes, cover and cook on MEDIUM (70%) for 5-7 minutes, stir in ground cumin, ground coriander, mango powder, turmeric and fresh coriander and cook on LOW (30%) for 2 minutes longer. Season to taste with salt.

Serves 6

LETTUCE AND DILL SALAD

$^1/_2$ lettuce, shredded
$^1/_2$ cucumber, scraped and thinly sliced
1 bunch fresh dill, coarsely chopped
2 tablespoons lemon juice
pinch paprika
salt

Place lettuce, cucumber, dill, lemon juice, paprika and salt to taste in a salad bowl and toss to combine.

Serves 6

Spicy Tomato with Bread

PLAIN RAITHA

1 cup/200 g/6¹/₂ oz natural yogurt
¹/₄ cup/60 mL/2 fl oz water
salt
freshly ground black pepper

Place yogurt, water, and salt and black pepper to taste in a bowl and beat to combine.

Makes 1 cup/250 mL/8 fl oz

VEGETARIAN MEAL

Clockwise from right: Lentils with Poori, Coriander and Mint Chutney, Tomato Yogurt, Eggplant with Tomatoes, Potato and Tomatoes

Panir with Fried
Bread Rolls
Panir Pau

Potato and Tomatoes
Allo Bhoji

Lentils with Poori
Dhal Poori

Eggplant with
Tomatoes

Chickpeas in
Onion Gravy
Chole Bhutora

Vegetables with
Spicy Rice
Sabzi Biryani

Tomato Yogurt
Tamatar Raitha

Coriander and Mint
Chutney
Kutmir Phudina Chutney

PANIR WITH FRIED BREAD ROLLS

1 bunch fresh coriander, leaves
removed and chopped

PANIR
8 cups/2 litres/3¹/₂ pt milk
1 cup/200 g/6¹/₂ oz natural yogurt
2 tablespoons lemon juice
salt

TOMATO SAUCE
1 tablespoon vegetable oil
2 teaspoons finely chopped fresh ginger
1 fresh red or green chilli,
finely chopped
1 teaspoon cumin seeds
2 tomatoes, chopped
¹/₄ teaspoon ground cumin
¹/₄ teaspoon ground coriander
pinch ground turmeric
pinch mango powder
8 Pau (fried bread rolls, see page 73)

The sauce will taste better if
you make it the day before
you plan to use it.
Rather than making your
own Panir, you can use
commercially available fresh
ricotta cheese. To use
purchased ricotta cheese in
this dish, simply follow the
instructions for draining as
described in the recipe.

1   To make Panir, place milk in a
saucepan and bring to the boil over a low
heat. Stir in yogurt, lemon juice and salt
to taste, then remove from heat. Stand for
2 minutes to allow the curds and whey to
separate. Line a colander with muslin or
gauze and set colander over a bowl. Pour
milk mixture into colander and set aside
to drain.

2   To make sauce, heat oil in a saucepan,
add ginger, chilli, cumin seeds and
tomatoes and cook, stirring, for 2 minutes.
Add Panir, ground cumin, ground
coriander, turmeric and mango powder
and mix well to combine. Just prior to
serving, sprinkle with fresh coriander.
Serve with Pau (fried bread rolls).

Serves 6

Potato and Tomatoes

$^1/_2$ teaspoon ground cumin
$^1/_2$ teaspoon ground coriander
$^1/_4$ teaspoon ground turmeric
$^1/_4$ teaspoon mango powder
2 tablespoons vegetable oil
2 teaspoons finely chopped fresh ginger
2 fresh red or green chillies,
finely chopped
1 teaspoon black mustard seeds
1 teaspoon cumin seeds
1 large sprig fresh curry leaves or
6-8 dried curry leaves
salt
4 potatoes, diced
1 cup/250 mL/8 fl oz water
4 large tomatoes, finely chopped

1   Place ground cumin, coriander, turmeric and mango powder in a small bowl and mix to combine. Set aside.

2   Heat oil in a heavy-based saucepan, add ginger, chillies, mustard seeds, cumin seeds, curry leaves and salt to taste, and cook over a low heat, stirring, for 2 minutes. Add potatoes, mix well and cook for 10 minutes. Add water and cook, stirring occasionally, for 10 minutes or until potatoes are almost cooked. Add tomatoes and cook, stirring occasionally, for 10 minutes or until tomatoes are pulpy. Stir in spice mixture and cook for 2 minutes longer.

To microwave: Place oil, ginger, chillies, mustard seeds, cumin seeds, curry leaves and salt to taste in a microwave-safe dish and cook on HIGH (100%) for 2 minutes. Add potatoes and water, mix well to combine and cook on HIGH (100%) for 10 minutes then on MEDIUM (70%) for 20 minutes or until potatoes are tender. Add tomatoes and cook on MEDIUM (70%) for 5 minutes longer. Stir in spice mixture and cook on LOW (30%) for 5 minutes.

Serves 6

Serve this dish with Lentils with Poori (see page 24).

Panir with Fried Bread Rolls: (in pan) cooking Pau (fried bread rolls); draining Panir; (in saucepan) Tomato Sauce

LENTILS WITH POORI

3 cups/750 mL/1$^{1}/_{4}$ pt water
2 cups/400 g/12$^{1}/_{2}$ oz mung dhal (small
yellow lentils), cleaned (see Mixed
Lentils page 30)
salt
2 teaspoons finely chopped fresh ginger
2 tablespoons vegetable oil
$^{1}/_{2}$ teaspoon ground turmeric
2 onions, thinly sliced
$^{1}/_{4}$ teaspoon paprika
$^{1}/_{4}$ teaspoon mango powder
$^{1}/_{4}$ teaspoon ground cumin
2 tablespoons chopped fresh coriander
16 Pooris (see page 74)

As lentils cook, skim any froth from the top, taking care not to put the spoon completely into lentil mixture. When the mixture boils, reduce heat and stir to prevent lentils catching and burning. Remove lid and continue to cook until mixture starts to thicken.

Serves 6

1   Place water in a large saucepan, add lentils, salt to taste, ginger, 1 tablespoon oil and turmeric and cook, partially covered, over a medium heat for 30 minutes. Beat with a hand beater, then reduce heat to the lowest possible setting and simmer for 10 minutes.

2   Heat remaining oil in a small frying pan, add onions and cook, stirring frequently, for 5 minutes or until onions are soft and golden.

3   Combine paprika, mango powder and cumin. To serve, spoon lentil mixture into a deep serving dish, top with onions and sprinkle with spice mixture and fresh coriander. Alternatively, press lentil mixture into a mould, then turn onto a serving plate. Serve with Pooris.

EGGPLANT WITH TOMATOES

16 baby eggplant (aubergines)
4 tablespoons vegetable oil
2 onions, chopped
2 fresh red or green chillies,
finely chopped
2 cloves garlic, finely chopped
2 teaspoons finely chopped fresh ginger
3 tomatoes, chopped
1 tablespoon lemon juice
$^{1}/_{4}$ teaspoon ground paprika
$^{1}/_{4}$ teaspoon ground cardamom
$^{1}/_{2}$ teaspoon ground cumin
$^{1}/_{2}$ teaspoon ground coriander
$^{1}/_{2}$ teaspoon mango powder
$^{1}/_{4}$ teaspoon ground turmeric
$^{1}/_{2}$ bunch coriander, leaves removed
and chopped

This dish is delicious served with Chapatis (see page 74).

1   Trim ends from eggplant (aubergines) and split lengthwise. Heat 2 tablespoons oil in a large frying pan, add eggplant (aubergines) and cook, turning frequently, until they start to soften. Remove eggplant (aubergines) from pan and drain on absorbent kitchen paper. Set aside.

2   Heat remaining oil in same frying pan, add onions, chillies, garlic and ginger and cook over a medium heat, stirring, for 5 minutes or until onions are golden. Stir in tomatoes, reduce heat to low and cook for 10 minutes or until tomatoes are soft and pulpy. Stir in lemon juice, paprika, cardamom, cumin, ground coriander, mango powder and turmeric and cook for 2 minutes longer. Stir in coriander.

3   To serve, spoon tomato mixture over eggplant (aubergines).

Serves 6

CHICKPEAS IN ONION GRAVY

440 g/14 oz dried chickpeas
$^1/_4$ teaspoon bicarbonate of soda
salt
2 onions, roughly chopped
2 teaspoons finely chopped fresh ginger
2 fresh red or green chillies,
finely chopped
2-3 cloves garlic, finely chopped
1 tablespoon vegetable oil
2 bay leaves
2 teaspoons whole cumin seeds
5 tomatoes, chopped
pinch garam masala
$^1/_2$ teaspoon ground coriander
$^1/_2$ teaspoon ground cumin
pinch mango powder
pinch ground fennel
pinch mace or nutmeg
pinch ground fenugreek
$^1/_2$ teaspoon ground turmeric

1   Place chickpeas, bicarbonate of soda and 1 teaspoon salt in a large bowl. Pour over enough water to cover. Cover and set aside to soak overnight.

2   Drain chickpeas and place in a saucepan. Cover with clean water, bring to the boil and boil for 10 minutes. Reduce heat and simmer for 1 hour or until chickpeas are tender. Drain and reserve cooking liquid.

3   Place 6 tablespoons cooked chickpeas, onions, ginger, chillies and garlic in a food processor or blender and process until smooth. Heat oil in a heavy-based frying pan, add onion mixture, bay leaves, cumin seeds and salt to taste and cook over a low heat, stirring frequently, for 30-40 minutes or until golden.

4   Stir in tomatoes and cook for 10-15 minutes longer or until tomatoes are soft and pulpy. Add remaining chickpeas, bring to the boil over a low heat, adding a little of reserved cooking liquid if mixture seems dry.

5   Combine garam masala, coriander, cumin, mango powder, fennel, mace or nutmeg, fenugreek and turmeric. Stir spice mixture into chickpea mixture and simmer for 5 minutes.

Serves 4

Serve this dish with Bhutoras (see page 73).

Chickpeas in Onion Gravy,
Spicy Vegetable Rice

Napkin Bay Tree Kitchen Shop Box Joan Bowers

VEGETABLES WITH SPICY RICE

Panir is Indian ricotta cheese. If you do not wish to make your own you can use commercially available fresh ricotta cheese in its place. To use purchased ricotta cheese in this dish, simply follow the instructions for draining and pressing as described in the recipe.

Do not be put off making this dish by the length of the recipe. As you will see, the Panir can be made in advance, and the rice and vegetable mixtures can also be made in advance. By preparing these components of the dish ahead, all you would need to do before the meal is to complete the recipe from step 6.

salt
vegetable oil
1^1/2 teaspoons ground cumin
1^1/2 teaspoons ground coriander
1^1/2 teaspoons ground cardamom
^{3}/4 teaspoon ground nutmeg
^{3}/4 teaspoon ground cloves
1^1/2 teaspoons mango powder
125 g/4 oz peas, blanched
250 g/8 oz cauliflower florets, blanched
pinch ground turmeric
^{1}/4 cup/60 mL/2 fl oz water
15 g/^{1}/2 oz ghee or butter
tandoori or red food colouring
2 drops green food colouring

PANIR
8 cups/2 litres/3^1/2 pt milk
1 cup/200 g/6^1/2 oz natural yogurt
2 tablespoons lemon juice

SPICE BAG
4 whole cloves
1 stick cinnamon, broken in half
5 green cardamom pods or 2 large cardamom pods
3 dried red whole chillies
2 bay leaves
^{3}/4 teaspoon coriander seeds
^{3}/4 teaspoon cumin seeds
^{1}/4 teaspoon black peppercorns
1 piece muslin, 12-15 cm/5-6 in square

SPICY RICE
^{1}/2 teaspoon cumin seeds
1 large onion, finely sliced
2 cups/440 g/14 oz rice
5 cups/1.2 litres/2 pt boiling water

GARNISH
1 teaspoon black cumin seeds
45 g/1^1/2 oz blanched almonds, toasted
2 large tomatoes, cut into thin wedges

1   To make Panir, place milk in a saucepan and bring to the boil over a low heat. Stir in yogurt, lemon juice and salt to taste, then remove from heat. Stand for 2 minutes to allow the curds and whey to separate. Line a colander with muslin or gauze and set colander over a bowl. Pour milk mixture into colander and set aside to drain. Fold muslin or gauze over Panir and place on a board, top with a second board, weight and set aside to drain for 10 minutes. Cut Panir into cubes and set aside.

2   To make Spice Bag, place cloves, cinnamon, cardamom pods, chillies, bay leaves, coriander seeds, cumin seeds and black peppercorns in the centre of the piece of muslin. Draw up corners and tie securely.

3   For rice, heat 2 tablespoons oil in a heavy-based saucepan, add cumin seeds, onion and salt to taste and cook over a medium heat until onion is soft and golden. Stir in rice and cook, stirring, for 2-3 minutes. Add Spice Bag and water and mix well. Bring to the boil, cover, reduce heat and simmer for 15 minutes or until rice is cooked. Remove Spice Bag and discard.

4   Place cumin, coriander, cardamom, nutmeg, cloves and mango powder in a bowl and mix to combine. Set aside.

5   Heat a little oil in a saucepan, add peas, salt to taste, one-third of the spice mixture and a little water, mix well and simmer for 5-7 minutes or until peas are just tender. In a separate saucepan, heat a little oil, add cauliflower, salt to taste, one-third of the spice mixture, a pinch of turmeric and water and simmer for 7-10 minutes or until cauliflower is just tender.

6 Heat 2 teaspoons oil and ghee or butter in a heavy-based frying pan, add Panir and cook until brown on both sides. Remove Panir from pan and place in a saucepan. Mix a pinch of tandoori or red food colouring with a little water, pour over Panir and simmer over a low heat for 5 minutes.

7 To serve, divide rice into three equal portions. Mix a pinch of tandoori or red food colouring with a little water and stir into one portion of rice. Mix pinch of turmeric with a little water and stir into another portion of rice, then mix green food colouring into remaining rice. Arrange vegetables and rice attractively on a large serving platter.

8 For garnish, heat 1 tablespoon oil in a small saucepan, add cumin seeds and allow to sizzle, remove from heat and pour over rice and vegetables. Cover dish with aluminium foil and bake for 10 minutes. Just prior to serving, sprinkle with almonds and sultanas. Surround with tomato wedges.

Serves 6

For a festive occasion, decorate this dish with silver leaf. Silver leaf is available from Indian specialty shops and some art supplies shops.

TOMATO YOGURT

1 cup/200 g/6$^{1}/_{2}$ oz natural yogurt
$^{1}/_{2}$ bunch fresh coriander, leaves removed and chopped
3 tomatoes, chopped
1 fresh green chilli, finely chopped
salt
freshly ground black pepper

Place yogurt in a bowl and whip until smooth. Add coriander, tomatoes, chilli, and salt and black pepper to taste. Mix well and serve.

Makes 1 cup/250 g/8 oz

CORIANDER AND MINT CHUTNEY

3 bunches fresh coriander, leaves removed
1 bunch fresh mint, leaves removed
6-8 fresh green chillies
3 teaspoons finely chopped fresh ginger
6 cloves garlic, finely chopped
2 tablespoons lemon juice
1 tablespoon caster sugar
$^{1}/_{4}$ cup/60 mL/2 fl oz water
salt

1 Place coriander leaves, mint leaves, chillies, ginger, garlic, lemon juice, sugar, water and salt to taste in a food processor or blender and process to a paste.

2 Spoon chutney into a sterilised jar, cover and refrigerate until ready to use.

Makes 1 x 250 g/8 oz jar

FORMAL MEAL

Mixed Lentils
Dhal

Fried Okra
Tali Bhindi

**Fresh Green
Vegetable Salad**
Hare Sabzi Sambal

Baked Fish
Masala Machi

Fresh Herb Raitha
Masala Raitha

Vegetable Pullao
Bhaji Pullao

China Bay Tree Kitchen Shop
Seat Joan Bowers

Clockwise from right: Fresh Green
Vegetable Salad, Fried Okra,
Baked Fish, Fresh Herb Raitha

MIXED LENTILS

45 g/1^1/$_2$ oz mung dhal
(small yellow lentils)
45 g/1^1/$_2$ oz channa dhal
(yellow split peas)
45 g/1^1/$_2$ oz thoor dhal
(medium flat yellow lentils)
45 g/1^1/$_2$ oz masoor dhal (pink lentils)
salt
2 tablespoons vegetable oil
^{1}/$_4$ teaspoon ground turmeric
2 fresh red or green chillies,
finely chopped
2 teaspoons finely chopped fresh ginger
^{1}/$_2$ teaspoon coriander seeds
1 teaspoon black mustard seeds
1 teaspoon fenugreek seeds
1 teaspoon yellow mustard seeds
1 teaspoon cumin seeds
2 branches fresh curry leaves or 12-16
dried curry leaves
^{1}/$_4$ teaspoon hing (asafoetida)
2 tablespoons concentrated tamarind
or 1 tablespoon tomato purée

Instead of the four types of lentils used in this dish you might wish to use just two or three types.
The unspiced lentil mixture freezes well, so you might like to cook double the quantity of lentils. Complete the recipe to the end of step 2, allow to cool, then freeze until required. When you want to use the lentils, simply defrost and complete the recipe as described.

Hing (asafoetida) is a hard block of resin. In India the block would be heated in a hot oven for 5 minutes, then ground to a fine powder. In the West it can be purchased already ground from Indian food shops. Hing is mainly used (in minute quantities) in dishes using lentils and pulses. It aids digestion and helps to prevent flatulence.

1 Pick lentils over and remove any small sticks or stones, then place lentils in a large bowl. Fill bowl with water and, using your hands, stir until water is cloudy. Drain and repeat until water is clear. You will probably need to repeat the procedure 3-4 times. Drain, pour over fresh water and set lentils aside to soak for 45 minutes.

2 Drain lentils and place in a saucepan with 2 cups/500 mL/16 fl oz of water, salt to taste, 1 tablespoon oil and turmeric and bring to the boil over a medium heat, reduce heat and simmer for 15 minutes or until lentils are soft. Place lentil mixture in a food processor or blender and process until smooth. Set aside.

3 Heat remaining oil in a large saucepan, add chillies, ginger, coriander seeds, mustard seeds, fenugreek seeds, yellow mustard seeds, cumin seeds and curry leaves and cook, stirring, for 1 minute. Add puréed lentil mixture and cook, stirring, for 2 minutes longer. Stir in 3 cups/750 mL/1^1/$_4$ pt hot water and bring to the boil. Add hing (asafoetida) and tamarind or tomato purée and cook for 2-5 minutes longer or until pulpy.

To microwave: Clean lentils as described in step 1. Place lentils, 2 cups/500 mL/ 16 fl oz boiling water, 1 tablespoon oil and turmeric in a large microwave-safe container, cover and cook on HIGH (100%) for 7 minutes, then on MEDIUM (70%) for 8 minutes. Reduce to LOW (30%) and cook for 5 minutes longer. Purée lentils and continue as for rest of recipe.

Serves 4

Mixed Lentils with uncooked lentils: (from top) thoor dhal, masoor dhal, mung dhal, channa dhal

FRIED OKRA

Rather than frying, you may prefer to cook the okra and spices together with 2 tablespoons of oil in a heavy-based frying pan over a low heat until tender.

Black salt is a spicy, pungent sulphurous rock. It adds a distinctive flavour and can be purchased ready-ground from Indian food shops.

vegetable oil for frying
500 g/1 lb okra, trimmed and cut
into 1 cm/^{1}/$_2$ in pieces
pinch caster sugar
pinch black salt
pinch paprika
pinch ground turmeric
pinch garam masala
^{1}/$_4$ teaspoon mango powder
^{1}/$_4$ teaspoon ground ginger
^{1}/$_4$ teaspoon ground cumin
^{1}/$_4$ teaspoon ground coriander
salt

1 Heat about 2.5 cm/1 in oil in a large frying pan, add okra and cook over a high heat until okra is crisp on the outside and tender inside. Remove okra from pan and drain on absorbent kitchen paper.

2 Combine caster sugar, black salt, paprika, turmeric, garam masala, mango powder, ginger, cumin, coriander and salt to taste. Transfer okra to a serving dish and sprinkle with spice mixture.

Serves 4

FRESH GREEN VEGETABLE SALAD

^{1}/$_2$ head lettuce, leaves separated
^{1}/$_2$ cucumber, peeled and sliced
1 avocado, stoned, peeled and sliced
2 stalks celery, sliced
100 g/3^1/$_2$ oz mung sprouts

LEMON DRESSING
2 tablespoons lemon juice
^{1}/$_2$ teaspoon paprika
^{1}/$_2$ teaspoon mango powder
^{1}/$_2$ teaspoon caster sugar
salt
freshly ground black pepper

1 Place lettuce, cucumber, avocado, celery and mung sprouts in a salad bowl.

2 To make dressing, place lemon juice, paprika, mango powder, sugar, and salt and black pepper to taste in a screwtop jar and shake well to combine. Spoon dressing over salad and toss to combine.

Serves 4

Fried Okra
Bowl Bay Tree Kitchen Shop

BAKED FISH

2 large onions, roughly chopped
1 tablespoon vegetable oil
2 cloves garlic, crushed
2 fresh red or green chillies,
finely chopped
2 teaspoons finely chopped fresh ginger
1 tablespoon cumin seeds
2 bay leaves
salt
4 large tomatoes, finely chopped
$^1/_2$ teaspoon ground cumin
$^1/_2$ teaspoon ground coriander
pinch ground cloves
pinch ground cinnamon
pinch ground cardamom
$^1/_2$ teaspoon mango powder
$^1/_4$ teaspoon ground turmeric
3 tablespoons cream (double)
4 firm white fish fillets, such as John
Dory or ocean perch
1 bunch fresh basil, leaves removed
and finely chopped

1   Place onions in a food processor or blender and process to make a purée.

2   Heat oil in a heavy-based saucepan, add garlic, chillies, ginger, cumin seeds, bay leaves, salt to taste and onion purée and cook over a medium heat until onions are a pinkish colour. Add tomatoes, ground cumin, coriander, cloves, cinnamon, cardamom, mango powder and turmeric and cook, stirring, for 3-4 minutes. Remove pan from heat and stir in cream.

3   Place fish in a baking dish, pour over sauce and bake for 20 minutes or until fish flakes when tested with a fork. Just prior to serving, sprinkle with basil.

Serves 4

Oven temperature
180°C, 350°F, Gas 4

This recipe is also delicious made with chicken fillets rather than fish. If using chicken, cook for 30 minutes.

The sauce may be made 24 hours ahead and kept in the refrigerator until you are ready to use it.

FRESH HERB RAITHA

1 cup/200 g/6$^1/_2$ oz natural yogurt
$^1/_4$ cup/60 mL/2 fl oz water
$^1/_4$ bunch fresh coriander, leaves
removed and coarsely chopped
2-3 large sprigs fresh mint, leaves
removed and coarsely chopped
2-3 large sprigs fresh basil, leaves
removed and coarsely chopped
2-3 large sprigs fresh dill,
coarsely chopped
12 fresh chives, snipped
salt

Place yogurt and water in a bowl and whip until smooth. Add coriander, mint, basil, dill, chives and salt to taste and mix to combine.

Makes 1$^1/_2$ cups/375 mL/12 fl oz

VEGETABLE PULLAO

Oven temperature
180°C, 350°F, Gas 4

500 g/1 lb mixed vegetables such as
peas, diced potatoes, sliced beans, diced
zucchini (courgette), diced carrot and
cauliflower florets
2 tablespoons vegetable oil
1 onion, sliced
1 bay leaf
1 cinnamon stick
$^1/_2$ teaspoon fennel seeds
$^1/_2$ teaspoon cumin seeds
$^1/_2$ teaspoon black mustard seeds
$^1/_2$ teaspoon yellow mustard seeds
$^1/_4$ teaspoon fenugreek seeds
2 teaspoons finely chopped fresh ginger
2 fresh red or green chillies,
finely chopped
2 cups/440 g/14 oz rice
5 cups/1.2 litres/2 pt hot water
2 hard-boiled eggs, sliced
2 tomatoes, sliced
silver leaf (optional)
60 g/2 oz salted cashews,
roughly chopped
90 g/3 oz sultanas

1   Boil, steam or microwave vegetables
until partially cooked. Drain and set
aside.

2   Heat oil in a large saucepan, add
onion, bay leaf, cinnamon stick, fennel
seeds, cumin seeds, black mustard seeds,
yellow mustard seeds, fenugreek seeds,
ginger and chillies and cook over a
medium heat for 1 minute.

3   Stir in rice and mix well to combine.
Add mixed vegetables and cook for 2
minutes. Stir in hot water and transfer
rice mixture to a casserole dish. Cover
and bake for 20-30 minutes or until rice is
cooked.

4   Place rice mixture on a large serving
platter. Decorate border with alternating
slices of egg and tomato, top rice with
silver leaf (if using), then sprinkle with
cashews and sultanas.

To microwave: Place oil, onion, bay leaf,
cinnamon stick, fennel seeds, cumin
seeds, black mustard seeds, yellow
mustard seeds, fenugreek seeds, ginger,
chillies, vegetables and $^1/_4$ cup/60 mL/
2 fl oz water in a microwave-safe dish.
Cover and cook on HIGH (100%) for
7 minutes. Stir in rice and cook on HIGH
(100%) for 3 minutes. Stir in hot water
and cook on HIGH (100%) for 15
minutes, then on LOW (30%) and cook
for 15 minutes longer. Serve as described
above.

Serves 4

When using silver leaf it must
be applied to the pullao
before other garnish
ingredients. The decorative
garnish is optional, but it
makes for an attractive
presentation.

Vegetable Pullao

Plate Bay Tree Kitchen Shop *Seat* Joan Bowers

INFORMAL MEAL

Beef Kofta in Cream
Sauce
Malai Kheema Kofta

Carrot and
Mandarin Salad

Mango Chutney
Aam Chutney

Mung Sprouts with
Spinach
Palak Mung

Spicy Rice
Masaladhar Chawal

Spicy Mixed
Vegetable Casserole
Masala Bhaji

Mixed Dry Spice
Yogurt
Sokhi Masala Raitha

Clockwise from right: Mung Sprouts with Spinach, Carrot and Mandarin Salad, Beef Kofta in Cream Sauce with Spicy Rice

China BayTree Kitchen Shop

BEEF KOFTA IN CREAM SAUCE

Chicken, lamb or veal mince
can be used in place of the
beef if you wish. Kofta is also
delicious eaten plain, without
a sauce.

The health-conscious can try
using English spinach in the
sauce in place of the cream.
You will need 2 bunches/
1 kg/2 lb English spinach.
Chop the spinach, then
steam or microwave until
tender. Drain, place in a
food processor or blender
and process until smooth.
Simply use the spinach purée
in place of the cream.

BEEF KOFTA

1 kg/2 lb beef mince
2 tablespoons cream (double)
2 teaspoons finely chopped fresh ginger
2 fresh red or green chillies,
finely chopped
3 cloves garlic, finely chopped
1 teaspoon mango powder
$1^{1}/_{2}$ teaspoons ground coriander
$1^{1}/_{2}$ teaspoons garam masala
$1^{1}/_{4}$ teaspoons ground cumin
salt

CREAM SAUCE

1 tablespoon vegetable oil
1 teaspoon cumin seeds
2 bay leaves
2 teaspoons finely chopped fresh ginger
2 fresh red or green chillies,
finely chopped
3 cloves garlic, finely chopped
300 mL/$9^{1}/_{2}$ fl oz cream (double)
1 teaspoon mango powder
$^{1}/_{2}$ teaspoon ground turmeric
$1^{1}/_{4}$ teaspoons ground coriander
$^{1}/_{2}$ teaspoon garam masala
$1^{1}/_{4}$ teaspoons ground cumin
1 bunch fresh coriander, leaves
removed and chopped

1 To make kofta, place mince, cream,
ginger, chillies, garlic, mango powder,
ground coriander, garam masala, cumin
and salt to taste in a bowl and mix well to
combine. Take spoonfuls of mixture and,
using wet hands, mould mixture into oval
shapes or rissoles and place in a steamer.
Three-quarters fill a saucepan with water
and bring to the boil. Place steamer over
saucepan, cover and steam for 15-20
minutes or until kofta is just cooked.

2 Remove kofta from steamer and place
in a shallow ovenproof dish. Set aside.

3 To make sauce, heat oil in a saucepan
over a low heat, add cumin seeds, bay
leaves, ginger, chillies and garlic and cook
for 2 minutes. Stir in cream, mango
powder, turmeric, ground coriander,
garam masala and cumin and cook,
stirring constantly, for 5-7 minutes.
Remove sauce from heat, stir in fresh
coriander and season to taste with salt.
Spoon sauce over kofta, cover and bake
for 20 minutes.

Serves 6

*Beef Kofta in Cream Sauce: (at back) steaming
kofta; (in bowl) Cream Sauce; (on plate)
uncooked kofta and spices*

CARROT AND MANDARIN SALAD

You might like to add a sliced
avocado to this salad.

2 mandarins, segmented,
all pith removed
2 carrots, grated
1 bunch fresh mint, leaves removed
and roughly chopped
2 tablespoons lemon juice
$^1/_4$ teaspoon paprika
$^1/_4$ teaspoon mango powder
$^1/_2$ teaspoon caster sugar
salt
freshly ground black pepper

1 Cut each mandarin segment in half
from top to bottom, making sure not to
cut right through. Open each segment to
form a circle and remove seeds. Arrange
mandarin segments attractively on a
serving platter.

If possible, make the dressing
1-2 hours in advance so that
the flavours have time to
develop.

2 Top mandarins with grated carrots
and sprinkle with chopped mint. Place
lemon juice, paprika, mango powder,
sugar, and salt and black pepper to taste
in a screwtop jar and shake well to
combine. Spoon lemon juice mixture
over salad and serve.

Serves 6

MANGO CHUTNEY

This recipe can easily be
doubled if you wish, but
remember to store the
chutney in the refrigerator.

250 g/8 oz raisins
2 x 440 g/14 oz canned mangoes,
drained and cut into cubes, or 4 ripe
mangoes, peeled and cut into cubes
$1^1/_2$ tablespoons finely chopped
fresh ginger
2 cloves garlic, finely chopped
3 teaspoons paprika
1 cinnamon stick
4 cloves
2 bay leaves
$^1/_2$ teaspoon mixed spice
3 tablespoons sultanas
$^1/_4$ cup/60 mL/2 fl oz cider vinegar
1-$1^1/_2$ cups/170-250 g/$5^1/_2$-8 oz
brown sugar

1 Place raisins in a small bowl, cover
with warm water and set aside to soak for
30 minutes. Drain.

2 Place mangoes, ginger, garlic, paprika,
cinnamon stick, cloves, bay leaves, mixed
spice, sultanas, vinegar, sugar and raisins
in a large heavy-based saucepan. Cover
and cook over a low heat, stirring
occasionally, for 1 hour or until chutney is
thick.

3 Spoon chutney into a warm sterilised
jar. Cover and label when cold. Store in
the refrigerator.

To microwave: Place mangoes, ginger,
garlic, paprika, cinnamon stick, cloves,
bay leaves, mixed spice, sultanas, vinegar,
sugar and raisins in a large microwave-safe
ceramic or glass container. Cover and
cook on HIGH (100%) for 15 minutes.
Stir and cook on MEDIUM (70%) for 15
minutes then on LOW (30%) for 10
minutes or until thick.

For a sweeter chutney use
the larger quantity of sugar;
for a less sweet chutney use
the smaller quantity.

Makes 1 x 250 g/8 oz jar

MUNG SPROUTS WITH SPINACH

1 tablespoon vegetable oil
1 teaspoon finely chopped fresh ginger
2 fresh red or green chillies,
finely chopped
1 teaspoon cumin seeds
1 teaspoon yellow mustard seeds
200 g/6^1/2 oz mung bean sprouts
2 tablespoons water
3 bunches/1.5 kg/3 lb English spinach,
leaves removed and chopped
^{1}/2 teaspoon ground turmeric
2 teaspoons lemon juice
salt

1   Heat oil in a wok or large frying pan, add ginger, chillies, cumin seeds and yellow mustard seeds and cook over a low heat, stirring, for 2-3 minutes.

2   Add mung bean sprouts and water and cook, stirring, for 5 minutes. Add spinach, turmeric, lemon juice and salt to taste and cook, stirring, for 5 minutes longer. Serve immediately.

Serves 6

This is one of the few Indian dishes that should be cooked just prior to serving.

SPICY RICE

5 cups/1.2 litres/2 pt water
2 cups/440 g/14 oz rice
1 teaspoon lemon juice
salt

SPICE BAG
^{1}/4 teaspoon black peppercorns
^{1}/4 teaspoon black onion seeds
^{1}/4 teaspoon cumin seeds
2 dried red chillies
1 cinnamon stick, broken in half
2 black cardamom pods
2 teaspoons finely chopped fresh ginger
2 bay leaves
1 piece muslin, 12-15 cm/5-6 in square

1   To make Spice Bag, place peppercorns, black onion seeds, cumin seeds, chillies, cinnamon, cardamom pods, ginger and bay leaves in the centre of the piece of muslin. Draw up corners and tie securely.

2   Place water in a large saucepan and bring to the boil. Stir in rice, lemon juice and salt to taste. Add Spice Bag and bring back to the boil, then reduce heat to low, cover and simmer for 12-15 minutes or until rice is cooked.

To microwave: Place water, rice, lemon juice, salt to taste and Spice Bag in a large microwave-safe container, cover and cook on HIGH (100%) for 8-10 minutes, then cook on MEDIUM (70%) for 10 minutes longer.

Serves 6

When using a Spice Bag you must make sure that it is securely tied otherwise the rice will have a bitter taste. The rice can be cooked in advance then reheated in the microwave on MEDIUM (70%) for 5-7 minutes.

SPICY MIXED VEGETABLE CASSEROLE

2 large onions, roughly chopped
2 large potatoes, diced
1 large carrot, diced
125 g/4 oz green beans, sliced
125 g/4 oz frozen peas or other diced
vegetables of your choice
2 tablespoons vegetable oil
1 cinnamon stick
2 teaspoons cumin seeds
1 teaspoon finely chopped fresh ginger
2 fresh red or green chillies,
finely chopped
2 bay leaves
1 teaspoon ground cumin
1 teaspoon ground coriander
1 teaspoon mango powder
$^1/_2$ teaspoon ground turmeric
salt

1   Place onions in a food processor or blender and process to make a purée. Set aside.

2   Place potatoes and carrot in a saucepan of water, bring to the boil, add beans and peas or other vegetables and cook for 10 minutes or until vegetables are just tender. Drain and reserve 2 cups/ 500 mL/16 fl oz cooking water. Refresh vegetables under cold running water and set aside.

3   Heat oil in a heavy-based saucepan, add cinnamon stick, cumin seeds, ginger, chillies and bay leaves and cook over a low heat, stirring, for 1 minute. Stir in onion purée, cover and cook, stirring occasionally, for 15-30 minutes or until mixture is a light brown colour.

4   Add cooked vegetables, reserved cooking water, ground cumin, coriander, mango powder, turmeric and salt to taste and cook, stirring occasionally, for 5 minutes.

To microwave: Place puréed onions, oil, cinnamon stick, cumin seeds, ginger, chillies and bay leaves in a microwave-safe container and cook on HIGH (100%) for 10 minutes. Stir well and cook on MEDIUM (70%) for 5 minutes longer. Add cooked vegetables, 1 cup/250 mL/ 8 fl oz reserved cooking water, ground cumin, coriander, mango powder and turmeric and cook on MEDIUM (70%) for 10-12 minutes. Season to taste with salt.

Serves 6

Tomatoes can be used in place of the onions in this dish if you wish. You will need 4 tomatoes. Finely chop the tomatoes and cook with the first quantity of spices for 10 minutes or until soft and pulpy. Complete as directed in the recipe.

*Spicy Mixed Vegetable Casserole,
Mixed Dry Spice Yogurt*

MIXED DRY SPICE YOGURT

1 cup/200 g/6^1/$_2$ oz natural yogurt
^{1}/$_4$ cup/60 mL/2 fl oz water
pinch salt
pinch paprika
pinch ground cumin
pinch ground coriander
pinch mango powder
pinch ground ginger
pinch black salt
pinch ground cardamom
^{1}/$_2$ bunch fresh coriander, leaves
removed and chopped

Place yogurt and water in a bowl and whip until smooth. Add salt, paprika, cumin, ground coriander, mango powder, ginger, black salt, cardamom and fresh coriander and mix to combine.

Makes 1 cup/250 mL/8 fl oz

Plate Bay Tree Kitchen Shop

OUTDOOR MEAL

Clockwise from right: Spicy Mushrooms with Panir, Apple Yogurt, Lamb Kebabs, Cabbage Salad

Lamb Kebabs
Ghosh Kebabs

Cabbage Salad
Pata Gobi Sambhal

Spicy Mushrooms
with Panir
Masala Khumbi Panir

Apple Yogurt
Sabi Raitha

Spiced Peas
and Carrots
Masala Peas Gajjar

Tamarind Chutney

LAMB KEBABS

1 kg/2 lb lamb cut into
2.5 cm/1 in cubes
salt
2 tablespoons lemon juice
2 cloves garlic, finely chopped
2 teaspoons finely chopped fresh ginger
2 fresh red chillies, finely chopped
1 teaspoon garam masala
1 teaspoon ground cumin
1 teaspoon ground coriander
1 teaspoon mango powder
$1/2$ teaspoon ground turmeric

TOMATO AND ONION SAUCE
3 large onions, roughly chopped
1 tablespoon vegetable oil
2 cloves garlic, finely chopped
2 teaspoons finely chopped fresh ginger
2 fresh red or green chillies,
finely chopped
3 large tomatoes, chopped
1 teaspoon garam masala
1 teaspoon ground cumin
1 teaspoon ground coriander
1 teaspoon mango powder
$1/2$ teaspoon ground turmeric
2 teaspoons cumin seeds
1 bunch fresh coriander, leaves
removed and chopped

1   Place lamb, salt to taste, lemon juice, garlic, ginger, chillies, garam masala, cumin, ground coriander, mango powder and turmeric in a bowl, mix to combine, cover and set aside to marinate for 2-3 hours.

2   Thread lamb onto twelve lightly oiled skewers and cook under a preheated medium grill, turning frequently, for 5-7 minutes or until just cooked.

3   To make sauce, place onions in a food processor or blender and process to form a purée. Heat oil in a heavy-based saucepan, add garlic, ginger and chillies and cook over a low heat, stirring, for 1 minute. Stir in onion purée and cook for 7-10 minutes or until onions are soft and slightly browned. Add tomatoes and cook for 10 minutes or until tomatoes are soft and pulpy. Stir in garam masala, ground cumin, ground coriander, mango powder, turmeric, cumin seeds and fresh coriander and cook for 5 minutes longer. Spoon sauce over kebabs.

Serves 4

In India this meal would be called *chatpati* (outdoor) or roadside meal. Indians love to have a quick snack when out shopping. Throughout India you will find roadside stalls where food is prepared on the spot by 'street hawkaro'. This is a typical *chatpati* that you can prepare yourself.

CABBAGE SALAD

$1/2$ small cabbage, shredded
1 tablespoon lemon juice
pinch paprika
pinch caster sugar
pinch salt
freshly ground black pepper
$1/2$ bunch fresh coriander, leaves
removed and chopped

1   Place cabbage in a flat bowl or dish.

2   Place lemon juice, paprika, sugar, salt and black pepper to taste in a screwtop jar and shake well to combine. Just prior to serving, spoon dressing over cabbage and toss to combine. Sprinkle with coriander and serve.

Serves 4

Spicy Mushrooms with Panir

1 tablespoon vegetable oil
1 slab Panir, cut into cubes (see page 26 for making Panir)
$1/4$ teaspoon ground cumin
$1/4$ teaspoon ground coriander
$1/4$ teaspoon mango powder
$1/4$ teaspoon caster sugar
$1/4$ teaspoon paprika
$1/4$ teaspoon ground turmeric
pinch black salt
30 g/1 oz butter
250 g/8 oz button mushrooms
$1/2$ bunch fresh coriander, leaves removed and chopped
salt

1   Heat oil in a large frying pan, add Panir and cook for 3-4 minutes each side or until golden. Remove Panir from pan and set aside.

2   Place cumin, ground coriander, mango powder, sugar, paprika, turmeric and black salt in a bowl and mix to combine.

3   Melt butter in a large clean frying pan, add mushrooms and cook for 2-3 minutes. Add Panir and cook over a low heat for 3-4 minutes longer. Remove pan from heat and stir in spice mixture, fresh coriander and salt to taste.

Serves 4

This dish can be reheated in the microwave on HIGH (100%) for 2 minutes.

If you do not wish to make your own Panir you can use purchased fresh ricotta cheese instead (see note on page 26).

Apple Yogurt

1 cup/200 g/$6^{1}/2$ oz natural yogurt
3-4 tablespoons water
salt
1 green apple, cored, peeled and grated
$1/4$ teaspoon ground cumin
$1/4$ teaspoon ground coriander
$1/4$ teaspoon paprika
$1/4$ teaspoon mango powder
2 teaspoons chopped fresh coriander
2 teaspoons chopped fresh mint

Place yogurt, water and salt to taste in a bowl and beat until smooth. Add apple, cumin, ground coriander, paprika and mango powder and mix well. Spoon into a serving dish and sprinkle with fresh coriander and mint.

Makes $1^{1}/2$ cups/375 mL/12 fl oz

SPICED PEAS AND CARROTS

250 g/8 oz frozen or shelled peas
2 carrots, diced
2 tablespoons vegetable oil
1 teaspoon cumin seeds
2 teaspoons finely chopped fresh ginger
2 fresh red or green chillies,
finely chopped
5-6 tablespoons water
salt

DRY SPICE MIXTURE
$^1/_4$ teaspoon ground cumin
$^1/_4$ teaspoon ground coriander
$^1/_4$ teaspoon mango powder
$^1/_4$ teaspoon ground turmeric

1   For spice mixture, place cumin, coriander, mango powder and turmeric in a small bowl, mix to combine and set aside.

2   Boil or microwave peas and carrots, separately, until just cooked. Drain, refresh under cold running water and set aside. Heat oil in a heavy-based saucepan over a low heat, add cumin seeds, ginger and chillies and cook, stirring, for 2-3 minutes. Add peas and carrots and mix to combine well. Stir in water and salt to taste and simmer for 5 minutes. Add spice mixture and simmer, stirring occasionally, for 5 minutes longer.

To microwave: Place peas, carrots, oil, cumin seeds, ginger, chillies and spice mixture in a microwave-safe dish. Cover and cook on MEDIUM (70%), stirring occasionally, for 20 minutes. Season to taste with salt.

Serves 4

When cooking this dish in the microwave, do not cook the peas and carrots first.

TAMARIND CHUTNEY

250 g/8 oz seedless dates, chopped
250 g/8 oz brown or palm sugar
155 g/5 oz tamarind
4 cups/1 litre/1$^3/_4$ pt water
1 tablespoon paprika
$^1/_2$ teaspoon cayenne pepper
2 teaspoons black salt
salt

1   Place dates, sugar, tamarind, water, paprika, cayenne pepper, black salt and salt to taste in a heavy-based saucepan, cover and bring to the boil over a medium heat. Reduce heat to low and cook, stirring occasionally, for 30-45 minutes or until mixture is soft and pulpy.

2   Remove pan from heat and set aside to cool for 10 minutes. Place mixture in a food processor and process, then push through a sieve. Spoon chutney into a warm sterilised jar. Cover and label when cold. Store in the refrigerator.

Makes 1 x 250 g/8 oz jar

Palm sugar is made from the sap of the palmyra palm. It is a coarse brown sugar that is sold in pieces and is used as a sweetener in Indian and Southeast Asian dishes. It is available from Indian and Asian food shops.

Tamarind Chutney: (in saucepan) cooking chutney;
(in bowl) dates; (at front) Tamarind Chutney;
(on board) tamarind, palm sugar, paprika and black salt

WEEKEND MEAL

Clockwise from right: Beans
Yogurt, Cauliflower with Pumpkin
Sauce, Tomato and Onion Salad,
Lamb in Spinach Sauce

Lamb in Spinach
Sauce
Palak Ghosh

Sesame Seed
Chutney
Til Chutney

Cauliflower with
Pumpkin Sauce
*Phool Gobi Aur
Kaddu Gravi*

Tomato and Onion
Salad
Cachumber

Diced Potato
with Fenugreek
Allo Bhaji Aur Methi-Ki-Sag

Beans Yogurt
Sem Raitha

LAMB IN SPINACH SAUCE

You can use 440 g/14 oz canned tomatoes, chopped, in place of the fresh tomatoes if you wish.

6 ripe tomatoes, roughly chopped
2 tablespoons vegetable oil
2 teaspoons finely chopped fresh ginger
3 fresh red or green chillies, finely chopped
3 cloves garlic, finely chopped
salt
500 g/1 lb diced lamb, finely chopped
$^1/_4$ teaspoon ground cumin
$^1/_4$ teaspoon ground coriander
$^1/_4$ teaspoon ground cinnamon
$^1/_4$ teaspoon ground cloves
$^1/_4$ teaspoon mango powder
$^1/_4$ teaspoon ground turmeric
3 bunches/1.5 kg/3 lb English spinach, finely chopped

1 Place tomatoes in a food processor or blender and process until smooth.

2 Heat oil in a heavy-based saucepan, add ginger, chillies, garlic and salt to taste and cook, stirring, for 2 minutes. Add lamb and mix well. Cover and cook over a low heat for 30-40 minutes or until lamb is tender.

3 Stir in tomatoes and cook for 10 minutes. Add cumin, coriander, cinnamon, cloves, mango powder and turmeric and cook over a low heat, stirring occasionally, for 10 minutes. Add spinach and cook for 5 minutes longer.

To microwave: Place oil, ginger, chillies, garlic and salt to taste in a microwave-safe dish, cover and cook on HIGH (100%) for 2 minutes. Add lamb, mix well, cover and cook on MEDIUM (70%) for 20 minutes. Stir in tomatoes, cumin, coriander, cinnamon, cloves, mango powder and turmeric and cook on MEDIUM (70%) for 15 minutes. Add spinach, mix to combine and cook on MEDIUM (70%) for 10 minutes longer or until lamb is tender.

Frozen spinach can be used to make this dish if fresh is unavailable.

Serves 4

SESAME SEED CHUTNEY

$^1/_2$ cup/75 g/2$^1/_2$ oz sesame seeds
1 bunch fresh coriander, leaves removed
1 bunch fresh mint, leaves removed
5 fresh green chillies
$^1/_4$ cup/60 mL/2 fl oz tamarind concentrate
6-7 tablespoons water
$^1/_2$ teaspoon salt

If tamarind concentrate is unavailable, 2 tablespoons tomato purée could be used in its place.

Place sesame seeds in a cast-iron frying pan and dry-fry over a low heat until dark brown in colour. Place sesame seeds in a food processor or blender and process to grind. Add coriander, mint, chillies, tamarind concentrate, water and salt and process to make a smooth paste. Spoon chutney into a sterilised jar, cover and label. Store in the refrigerator.

Makes 1 x 125 g/4 oz jar

CAULIFLOWER WITH PUMPKIN SAUCE

1 cauliflower, broken into florets,
stems removed
1 butternut pumpkin, grated
2 tablespoons vegetable oil
$^1/_4$ cup/60 mL/2 fl oz water
$^1/_4$ teaspoon ground cumin
$^1/_4$ teaspoon ground coriander
$^1/_4$ teaspoon ground turmeric
$^1/_4$ teaspoon mango powder
2 teaspoons finely chopped fresh ginger
2 fresh red or green chillies,
finely chopped
salt
$^1/_2$ bunch fresh coriander, leaves
removed and finely chopped

1   Steam or microwave cauliflower and pumpkin, separately, until just tender. Drain cauliflower and refresh under cold water and set aside. Drain pumpkin, place in a food processor or blender and process to form a purée. Set aside.

2   Heat 1 tablespoon oil in a wok or large frying pan, add cauliflower, water, cumin, ground coriander, turmeric and mango powder and cook, stirring frequently, for 5-7 minutes. Transfer cauliflower mixture to an ovenproof dish and set aside.

3   Heat remaining oil in a saucepan, add ginger and chillies and cook, stirring, for 1 minute. Add pumpkin purée and cook over a low heat for 5 minutes. Season to taste with salt. Pour pumpkin mixture over cauliflower, sprinkle with fresh coriander and bake for 30 minutes.

To microwave: Place 1 tablespoon oil, cauliflower, cumin, ground coriander, turmeric and mango powder in a microwave-safe dish. Cover and cook on HIGH (100%) for 10 minutes. Place remaining oil, ginger, chillies and puréed pumpkin in a separate microwave-safe dish and cook on HIGH (100%) for 5 minutes. Season to taste with salt. Pour pumpkin mixture over cauliflower, cover and cook on MEDIUM (70%) for 7-8 minutes.

Serves 4

Oven temperature
150°C, 300°F, Gas 2

Any pumpkin can be used to make this sauce but butternut pumpkin gives a sweeter flavour and a smoother texture.

The sauce can be made several hours ahead of time, but should only be added to the cauliflower just prior to baking.
You might like to try serving the sauce as an accompaniment to other foods. It goes particularly well with grilled lamb cutlets or boiled baby new potatoes.

Sesame Seed Chutney
Bay Tree Kitchen Shop

TOMATO AND ONION SALAD

1 onion, sliced
1 tomato, sliced
salt
1 tablespoon lemon juice
$^1/_4$ bunch fresh coriander, leaves
removed and chopped

Place onion, tomato and salt to taste in a bowl, pour over lemon juice and sprinkle with coriander. Toss to combine and serve.

Serves 4

DICED POTATO WITH FENUGREEK

2 tablespoons vegetable oil
$^1/_2$ teaspoon cumin seeds
$^1/_2$ teaspoon yellow mustard seeds
2 teaspoons finely chopped fresh ginger
3 fresh red or green chillies,
finely chopped
salt
185 g/6 oz diced potatoes
$^1/_2$ cup/125 mL/4 fl oz water
2-3 tablespoons dried fenugreek leaves,
washed and drained or 1 teaspoon
ground fenugreek
$^1/_4$ teaspoon ground cumin
$^1/_4$ teaspoon ground coriander
$^1/_4$ teaspoon ground turmeric
$^1/_4$ teaspoon mango powder
$^1/_2$ bunch fresh coriander, leaves
removed and chopped finely

1   Heat oil, cumin seeds, yellow mustard seeds, ginger, chillies and salt to taste in a heavy-based saucepan. Add potatoes and cook over a medium heat, stirring constantly, for 5 minutes. Add water, cover and cook over a low heat for 5 minutes or until potatoes are half-cooked.

2   Stir in fenugreek leaves, ground cumin, ground coriander, turmeric and mango powder and cook for 5-10 minutes or until potatoes are cooked. Just prior to serving, sprinkle with fresh coriander.

To microwave: Place oil, cumin seeds, mustard seeds, ginger, chillies, potatoes and $^1/_4$ cup/60 mL/2 fl oz water in a microwave-safe dish. Cover and cook on HIGH (100%) for 20 minutes. Add fenugreek leaves, ground cumin, ground coriander, turmeric and mango powder and cook on MEDIUM (70%) for 15 minutes longer or until potatoes are cooked. Season to taste with salt. Just prior to serving, sprinkle with fresh coriander.

Serves 4

Buy fenugreek leaves in small quantities only, as required, to ensure their freshness and flavour.

Beans Yogurt

200 g/6¹/₂ oz snake or green beans,
chopped into 5 mm/¹/₄ in lengths
¹/₂ teaspoon finely chopped fresh ginger
1 small fresh red or green chilli,
finely chopped
15 g/¹/₂ oz butter
salt
1 cup/200 g/6¹/₂ oz natural yogurt
¹/₂ bunch fresh coriander, leaves
removed and finely chopped

DRY SPICE MIXTURE
pinch black salt
pinch mango powder
pinch ground cumin
pinch ground coriander
pinch ground turmeric

1   Combine beans, ginger, chilli, butter
and salt to taste and steam or microwave
until beans are tender. Drain, transfer to a
shallow dish and set aside to cool.

2   For spice mixture, combine black salt,
mango powder, cumin, ground coriander
and turmeric. Place yogurt and spice
mixture in a bowl and beat until smooth.
Spoon yogurt mixture over beans and mix
to combine. Just prior to serving, sprinkle
with fresh coriander.

Serves 4

Diced Potato with Fenugreek

BANQUET

Veal Pullao
Shahi Ghosh Pullao

Thoor Lentils
Thoor Dhal

Lentil and Rice
Dumplings
Dahi Bada

Fried Okra and
Potatoes
Tahi Bhindhi Allo

Fresh Herb Pullao
Masala Pullao

Gujarati-style Beans
Gujarati Beans

Delhi Salad
Delhi Sambal

Meat Kebabs with
Yogurt
Dahi Kofta

Clockwise from right: Delhi Salad with Gujarati-style Beans, Veal Pullao, Thoor Lentils, Fried Okra and Potatoes

Sari Joan Bowers

VEAL PULLAO

Oven temperature
180°C, 350°F, Gas 4

3 tablespoons vegetable oil
salt
750 g/1¹/₂ lb veal or lamb fillets
4 cups/1 litre/1³/₄ pt water
2 onions, thinly sliced
2 teaspoons chopped fresh ginger
5 cloves garlic, chopped
2 fresh green chillies, finely chopped
¹/₂ teaspoon ground cumin
¹/₂ teaspoon ground cardamom
¹/₂ teaspoon ground nutmeg
¹/₂ teaspoon ground cloves
pinch turmeric
2¹/₂ cups/500 g/1 lb natural yogurt

SPICE BAGS
8 cloves
2 sticks cinnamon
12 green cardamom pods or 2 large
black cardamom pods
6 dried red chillies
4 bay leaves
¹/₂ teaspoon coriander seeds
¹/₂ teaspoon cumin seeds
¹/₂ teaspoon black peppercorns
2 pieces muslin, each 12-15 cm/
5-6 in square

RICE
2 cups/440 g/14 oz rice
pinch tandoori colouring or
red food colouring
pinch turmeric
2 drops green food colouring

GARNISH
1 tablespoon vegetable oil
1¹/₂ teaspoons black cumin seeds
silver leaf (optional)
30 g/1 oz fried blanched almond slivers
30 g/1 oz fried or salted cashews
155 g/5 oz chopped pistachios
45 g/1¹/₂ oz fried sultanas
2 onions, sliced and fried
3 hard-boiled eggs, thinly sliced
2 tablespoons chopped fresh coriander
1 lemon, cut into wedges (optional)

1   To make Spice Bags, place half the cloves, cinnamon sticks, cardamom pods, chillies, bay leaves, coriander seeds, cumin seeds and black peppercorns on each piece of muslin. Draw up corners and tie securely. Set aside.

2   Heat 1 tablespoon oil, salt to taste and 1 spice bag in a large deep saucepan. Add veal or lamb fillets and water and bring to the boil over a high heat. Remove meat and spice bag. Pat meat dry and set aside. Strain cooking liquid and reserve for cooking rice.

3   Heat remaining oil in a large frying pan, add onions, ginger, garlic and chillies and cook over a medium heat, stirring, for 10 minutes or until onions are soft. Stir in cumin, cardamom, nutmeg, cloves and turmeric. Transfer onion mixture to a bowl, stir in yogurt and 2 tablespoons water and set aside.

4   Heat the same frying pan over a high heat, add veal or lamb fillets and cook quickly on all sides to seal. Remove fillets and place in a baking dish. Spoon yogurt mixture over fillets, cover and refrigerate for 4 hours.

5   Remove cover from baking dish and bake for 1 hour for veal or 30 minutes for lamb, or cook in the microwave on MEDIUM (70%) for 35 minutes for veal or 20 minutes for lamb.

6   To cook rice, place rice in an ovenproof dish. Measure reserved cooking liquid and add enough water to make up 5 cups /1.2 litres/2 pt liquid. Add to rice with remaining spice bag and salt to taste and bake at 160°C/325°F/Gas 3 for 45 minutes or cook in the microwave on HIGH (100%) for 20 minutes. Divide rice into four portions. Mix tandoori colouring with a little water and mix into one portion of rice to make red-coloured

Veal Pullao is a dish that should be made at a leisurely pace. It is not the sort of dish to attempt when time is short.

rice. Mix turmeric with a little water and mix into a second portion of rice to make yellow-coloured rice. Mix green food colouring with a little water and mix into third portion of rice to make green rice. Leave remaining portion of rice plain.

7   To serve, place veal with juices in centre of a large flat platter. Surround with mounds of rice. For the garnish, heat 1 tablespoon oil in a soup ladle and pour

in black cumin seeds. Allow to sizzle then remove from heat and pour over rice. Top rice with silver leaf (if using) then sprinkle with almonds, cashews, pistachios, sultanas and onions. Cover veal with egg slices and sprinkle with fresh coriander. Surround with lemon wedges (if using) and serve.

Serves 8

THOOR LENTILS

8 cups/2 litres/3^1/$_2$ pt water
2 cups/400 g/12^1/$_2$ oz thoor dhal
(medium flat yellow lentils), cleaned
and soaked
2 tablespoons vegetable oil
1 teaspoon cumin seeds
8-10 dried curry leaves
1 teaspoon yellow mustard seeds
1 teaspoon fenugreek seeds
2 teaspoons finely chopped fresh ginger
2 fresh red or green chillies,
finely chopped
salt
^{1}/$_2$ bunch fresh coriander, leaves
removed and chopped

1   Place 4 cups/1 litre/1^3/$_4$ pt water in a large saucepan and bring to the boil. Stir in lentils and 1 tablespoon oil, reduce heat to low and simmer, stirring frequently and removing froth, for 10-15 minutes or until lentils are soft and pulpy.

2   Heat remaining oil in a heavy-based saucepan, add cumin seeds, curry leaves, yellow mustard seeds, fenugreek seeds, ginger and chillies and cook over a low heat for 2-3 minutes. Stir in cooked lentils and remaining water and bring to the boil. Remove pan from heat, season lentil mixture to taste with salt and sprinkle with fresh coriander.

To microwave: Place lentils in a microwave-safe dish, pour over 4 cups/ 1 litre/1^3/$_4$ pt boiling water and cook on HIGH (100%) for 8 minutes, then on MEDIUM (70%) for 10 minutes longer. If the lentils are not completely cooked, continue to cook on LOW (30%) for 8-10 minutes longer or until cooked. Complete as for step 2 above.

Serves 8

The unspiced lentil mixture can be cooked in advance and frozen until required.

LENTIL AND RICE DUMPLINGS

$1^1/2$ cups/185 g/6 oz white urad
dhal flour
$1/2$ cup/90 g/3 oz ground rice
(fine rice flour)
4 fresh green chillies, finely chopped
1 teaspoon finely chopped fresh ginger
$1/4$ teaspoon bicarbonate of soda
2 teaspoons sultanas
2 teaspoons chopped salted cashews
2 teaspoons chopped blanched almonds
salt
1 bunch fresh coriander, leaves
removed and chopped
water
vegetable oil for deep-frying
1 cup/200 g/6$1/2$ oz natural yogurt
$1/4$ teaspoon mango powder
$1/4$ teaspoon ground cumin
$1/4$ teaspoon ground coriander
$1/4$ teaspoon paprika
$1/4$ teaspoon black salt
1 tablespoon black mustard seeds
5-7 fresh or dried curry leaves

1   Place dhal flour, ground rice (fine rice flour), chillies, ginger, bicarbonate of soda, sultanas, cashews, almonds, salt to taste and half the fresh coriander in a bowl. Stir in enough water to make a thick smooth batter, mix well to combine, cover and set aside to stand for 1 hour.

2   Heat oil in a wok, until a cube of bread dropped in browns in 50 seconds. Scoop a spoonful of batter into the palm of your hand and gently pat to form a dumpling. Cook 4-5 dumplings at a time in hot oil until golden.

3   Using a slotted spoon, remove dumplings from oil and drop into a bowl of warm water. Allow dumplings to soak for 5-7 minutes, then remove and squeeze between the palms of your hands to flatten and remove excess water. Arrange dumplings on a flat serving dish.

4   Place yogurt and $1/4$ cup/60 mL/2 fl oz water in a bowl and beat until smooth. Spoon a little yogurt mixture over each dumpling to completely cover.

5   Combine mango powder, cumin, ground coriander, paprika and black salt and set aside. Remove 2 tablespoons of hot oil from wok, place in a metal ladle and heat over a low heat. Add black mustard seeds and curry leaves and continue to heat until they sizzle. Pour oil mixture evenly over dumplings, then sprinkle with spice mixture and remaining fresh coriander. Serve immediately.

Serves 8

White urad dhal flour is made from white split gram beans. Ground rice is also called rice flour. Both white urad dhal flour and ground rice are available from Asian and Indian food shops.

Lentil and Rice Dumplings: (at back) dumplings soaking in warm water and dumplings squeezed to remove excess water

Dishes Bay Tree Kitchen Shop

FRIED OKRA AND POTATOES

vegetable oil for deep-frying
250 g/8 oz okra, trimmed and sliced
into 5 mm/^{1}/$_4$ in rounds
250 g/8 oz potatoes, diced
^{1}/$_4$ teaspoon ground cumin
^{1}/$_4$ teaspoon ground coriander
^{1}/$_4$ teaspoon ground ginger
^{1}/$_4$ teaspoon paprika
^{1}/$_4$ teaspoon caster sugar
^{1}/$_4$ teaspoon mango powder
salt
1 bunch fresh coriander, leaves
removed and chopped

1   Heat oil in a wok until a cube of bread dropped in browns in 50 seconds. Add okra and potatoes and deep-fry for 5-7 minutes or until okra are crisp with brown edges and potatoes are golden and cooked through. Remove okra and potatoes and drain on absorbent kitchen paper.

2   Place okra and potatoes in a serving dish. Combine cumin, ground coriander, ginger, paprika, sugar, mango powder and salt to taste. Add spice mixture and fresh coriander to vegetable mixture and toss to combine.

Serves 8

If fresh okra is unavailable, frozen okra can be used for this recipe. Frozen okra is available from Indian and Middle Eastern food shops.

FRESH HERB PULLAO

2 tablespoons vegetable oil
1 teaspoon cumin seeds
1 teaspoon black mustard seeds
^{1}/$_2$ teaspoon fennel seeds
^{1}/$_4$ teaspoon fenugreek seeds
1 stick cinnamon
2 cardamom pods, bruised
2 bay leaves
1 fresh red or green chilli,
finely chopped
2 teaspoons finely chopped fresh ginger
salt
2 cups/440 g/14 oz rice
1 tablespoon lemon juice
2 tablespoons chopped fresh coriander
2 tablespoons chopped fresh dill
1 tablespoon chopped fresh mint
1 tablespoon chopped fresh basil
1 tablespoon snipped fresh chives
4 cups/1 litre/1^3/$_4$ pt water

Heat oil in a heavy-based saucepan. Add cumin seeds, mustard seeds, fennel seeds, fenugreek seeds, cinnamon stick, cardamom pods, bay leaves, chilli, ginger and salt to taste and cook, stirring, for 2 minutes. Stir in rice, lemon juice, coriander, dill, mint, basil, chives and water and bring to the boil. Reduce heat to low, cover and simmer for 15-20 minutes or until cooked.

To microwave: Place oil, cumin seeds, mustard seeds, fennel seeds, fenugreek seeds, cinnamon stick, cardamom pods, bay leaves, chilli, ginger, salt to taste, rice, lemon juice, coriander, dill, mint, basil and chives in a large microwave-safe dish. Stir in 4 cups/1 litre/1^3/$_4$ pt water and cook on HIGH (100%) for 8-10 minutes, then on MEDIUM (70%) for 10-12 minutes or until rice is cooked.

Serves 8

The Fruit Chutney on page 69 makes a delicious accompaniment to this meal.

Meat Kebabs with Yogurt, Fresh Herb Pullao

Pewter dish Bay Tree Kitchen Shop

Gujarati-style Beans

3 tablespoons vegetable oil
3 teaspoons finely chopped fresh ginger
1-2 fresh red or green chillies,
finely chopped
salt
500 g/1 lb green beans, chopped
$^1/_2$ cup/125 mL/4 fl oz water
1 teaspoon ground coriander
1 teaspoon ground cumin
1 teaspoon mango powder
1 teaspoon caster sugar
$^1/_4$ teaspoon ground turmeric
$^1/_2$ teaspoon black mustard seeds
30 g/1 oz grated fresh or
desiccated coconut
1 bunch fresh coriander, leaves
removed and chopped
1 tablespoon lemon juice

1   Heat 2 tablespoons oil in a heavy-
based saucepan over a medium heat. Add
ginger, chillies and salt to taste and allow
to sizzle for 1 minute. Add beans and
water, stir well to combine, then reduce
heat and cook for 10 minutes.

2   Stir in ground coriander, cumin,
mango powder, sugar and turmeric and
cook, stirring occasionally, for 4-5
minutes or until beans are tender.
Transfer beans to a serving dish.

3   Heat remaining oil in a metal ladle,
add black mustard seeds to oil and when
they start to sizzle and pop, pour over the
beans. Sprinkle beans with coconut, fresh
coriander and lemon juice.

To microwave: Place 2 tablespoons oil,
ginger, chillies, beans and $^1/_4$ cup/60 mL/
2 fl oz water in a microwave-safe dish,
cover and cook on MEDIUM (70%) for
10 minutes. Stir in coriander, cumin,
mango powder, sugar, turmeric and salt to
taste, cover and cook on MEDIUM
(70%) for 10 minutes longer. Complete
as in step 3 above.

Serves 8

Delhi Salad

$^1/_2$ cup/125 mL/4 fl oz light sesame seed
or light vegetable oil
$^1/_2$ cup/125 mL/4 fl oz cream (double)
4 tablespoons lemon juice
1 teaspoon finely chopped garlic
1 teaspoon finely chopped ginger
$^1/_4$ teaspoon ground cumin
1 tablespoon caster sugar
salt
2 cucumbers, diced
4 radishes, diced
5 small potatoes, cooked and diced
2 fresh green chillies, chopped
1 slab Panir, cut into cubes (see page 26
for making Panir)
1 bunch fresh coriander, leaves removed
and coarsely chopped
3 tomatoes, chopped

1   Place oil, cream, lemon juice, garlic,
ginger, cumin, sugar and salt to taste in a
bowl and whisk to combine. Cover and
refrigerate for 2-3 hours before serving.

2   Place cucumbers, radishes, potatoes,
chillies, Panir, coriander and tomatoes in
a bowl. Spoon over half the dressing and
toss to combine. Reserve remaining
dressing for another use.

Serves 8

The dressing will keep in the
refrigerator for 2-3 days.

MEAT KEBABS WITH YOGURT

1 cup/200 g/6^1/$_2$ oz natural yogurt
^{1}/$_4$ cup/60 mL/2 fl oz water
^{1}/$_2$ bunch fresh coriander, leaves
removed and chopped

MEAT KEBABS
500 g/1 lb veal, lamb, beef or
chicken mince
^{1}/$_4$ teaspoon ground cloves
^{1}/$_4$ teaspoon ground cinnamon
^{1}/$_4$ teaspoon ground cardamom
^{1}/$_4$ teaspoon ground nutmeg
^{1}/$_2$ teaspoon ground cumin
^{1}/$_2$ teaspoon ground coriander
^{1}/$_2$ teaspoon mango powder
^{1}/$_2$ teaspoon paprika
^{1}/$_2$ teaspoon ground ginger
salt
200 mL/6^1/$_2$ fl oz cream (double)
1 egg
1 bunch fresh coriander, leaves
removed and chopped
vegetable oil for deep-frying

DRY SPICE GARNISH
^{1}/$_4$ teaspoon mango powder
^{1}/$_4$ teaspoon paprika
^{1}/$_4$ teaspoon caster sugar
^{1}/$_4$ teaspoon black salt

1 To make kebabs, place mince, cloves, cinnamon, cardamom, nutmeg, cumin, ground coriander, mango powder, paprika, ginger and salt to taste in a bowl and knead well for about 5 minutes. Add cream, 1 tablespoon at a time, kneading mince mixture well after each addition. Break egg into mince mixture and knead for 5 minutes longer. Set aside to stand for 15 minutes. Add fresh coriander to mince mixture and knead for 5 minutes. Take small portions of mince mixture and, using wet hands, form into oval-shaped kebabs about 5 cm/2 in long.

2 Place kebabs in a steamer set over a wok or saucepan of simmering water and steam for 15-25 minutes or until cooked. Remove kebabs from steamer and set aside.

3 Heat 2.5 cm/1 in oil in a heavy-based frying pan and cook kebabs quickly until golden. Transfer kebabs to a serving dish, set aside and keep warm.

4 Place yogurt and water in a bowl and beat until smooth. Spoon yogurt mixture over kebabs.

5 For garnish, combine mango powder, paprika, sugar, black salt and salt to taste. Sprinkle spice mixture and fresh coriander over kebabs.

Serves 8

This meal is a banquet to serve eight; however from this mince you could make two meals, each of which would serve four. The following dishes would combine well to give a smaller meal: Veal Pullao, Gujarati-style Beans, Delhi Salad and Lentil and Rice Dumplings. Another meal might consist of the following dishes: Meat Kebabs with Yogurt, Fried Okra and Potatoes, Fresh Herb Pullao and Fruit Chutney (page 69).

MOGUL MEAL

Mogul Lamb
Moglai Ghosh

Mogul Salad
Moglai Sambal

Fruit Chutney
Phal Chutney

Red Lentils
Masoor Dhal

Rice with Peas
and Spices
Peas Pullao

*Mogul Salad, Red Lentils,
Mogul Lamb*

Tableware and Fabric Joan Bowers

MOGUL LAMB

Oven temperature
180°C, 350°F, Gas 4

A quicker version of this dish uses 1 kg/2 lb diced lamb, rather than a leg. Heat butter in a saucepan with chillies, ginger, garlic and salt to taste. Add diced lamb and cook over a low heat for 30-40 minutes. Add black pepper, cardamom, cloves, fennel, cinnamon and fenugreek and cook for 10 minutes. Stir in tomatoes and cook for 20-30 minutes or until lamb is tender. Add coriander, basil, mint and dill and cook for 5 minutes longer. Serve with rice or Parathas (see page 75).

15 g/¹/₂ oz butter
750 g/1/¹/₂ lb ripe tomatoes,
finely chopped
2-3 fresh red or green chillies,
finely chopped
2 teaspoons finely chopped fresh ginger
4 cloves garlic, finely chopped
salt
1 teaspoon freshly ground black pepper
¹/₂ teaspoon ground cardamom
¹/₂ teaspoon ground cloves
¹/₂ teaspoon ground fennel
¹/₂ teaspoon ground cinnamon
¹/₂ teaspoon ground fenugreek
¹/₂ cup/125 mL/4 fl oz water
2 bunches fresh coriander, leaves
removed and chopped
¹/₄ bunch fresh basil, leaves
removed and chopped
¹/₂ bunch fresh mint, leaves
removed and chopped
¹/₄ bunch fresh dill, chopped
1 x 1.5 kg/3 lb leg lamb

1   Melt butter in a large saucepan, add tomatoes, chillies, ginger, garlic and salt to taste and cook over a medium heat, stirring frequently, for 15 minutes or until tomatoes are soft and pulpy.

2   Place black pepper, cardamom, cloves, fennel, cinnamon, fenugreek and water in a bowl and mix well to combine. Stir spice mixture into tomato mixture then add coriander, basil, mint and dill. Remove sauce from heat and set aside. Place lamb in a glass or ceramic baking dish, pour over sauce, cover and marinate in the refrigerator for 15-20 hours.

3   Remove cover from baking dish and bake lamb for 2 hours or until cooked to your liking.

Serves 6

MOGUL SALAD

200 g/6¹/₂ oz mung bean sprouts
3 cucumbers, diced
4 teaspoons grated fresh or
desiccated coconut
2 tomatoes, diced
¹/₄ bunch fresh coriander, leaves
removed and chopped
¹/₂ bunch fresh mint, leaves
removed and chopped
¹/₂ bunch fresh basil, leaves
removed and chopped
1 bunch spring onions, chopped
2 tablespoons lemon juice
salt
freshly ground black pepper

Place bean sprouts, cucumbers, coconut, tomatoes, coriander, mint, basil, spring onions, lemon juice, and salt and black pepper to taste in a bowl and toss to combine. Cover and stand at room temperature for 2-3 hours before serving.

Serves 6

FRUIT CHUTNEY

125 g/4 oz dried peaches, chopped
125 g/4 oz dried apricots, chopped
500 g/1 lb Granny Smith apples, cored,
peeled and chopped
2 teaspoons finely chopped fresh ginger
100 g/3$^{1}/_{2}$ oz sultanas
2 cups/500 mL/16 fl oz white vinegar
2 teaspoons salt
400 g/12$^{1}/_{2}$ oz caster sugar
5 cloves garlic, finely chopped
$^{3}/_{4}$ teaspoon cayenne pepper (optional)

1   Place peaches, apricots, apples, ginger, sultanas, vinegar, salt, sugar, garlic and cayenne pepper (if using) in a large heavy-based saucepan. Cover and cook over a low heat, stirring occasionally, for 1$^{1}/_{2}$ hours or until mixture is soft and pulpy.

2   Spoon chutney into hot sterilised jars. When cold, cover and label. Store in the refrigerator.

To microwave: Place peaches, apricots, apples, ginger, sultanas, vinegar, salt, sugar, garlic and cayenne pepper (if using) in a large glass or ceramic microwave-safe dish. Cover and cook on HIGH (100%), stirring occasionally, for 15 minutes, then on MEDIUM (70%) for 15 minutes and finally on LOW (30%) for 15 minutes or until chutney is thick.

Makes 2 x 250 g/8 oz jars

Fruit Chutney
Bowl Joan Bowers

69

RED LENTILS

water
1 1/2 cups/300 g/9 1/2 oz red lentils,
cleaned and soaked
1 teaspoon vegetable oil
1 teaspoon finely chopped fresh ginger
1/4 teaspoon ground turmeric
salt

TOMATO AND ONION SAUCE
2 tablespoons vegetable oil
2 teaspoons finely chopped fresh ginger
2 fresh red or green chillies, chopped
3 onions, minced
4 tomatoes, diced
30 g/1 oz ghee or butter
1/4 teaspoon cumin seeds
1/4 teaspoon fennel seeds
1/4 teaspoon black mustard seeds
1/4 teaspoon fenugreek seeds
1/4 teaspoon black onion seeds
3 dried red chillies
2 bay leaves
2 teaspoons garlic paste (optional)

1   Place 2 cups/500 mL/16 fl oz water in a saucepan and bring to the boil. Add lentils, 1 teaspoon oil, ginger, turmeric and salt to taste and cook, partially covered, for 10-15 minutes or until lentils are soft and pulpy.

2   To make sauce, heat oil in a heavy-based saucepan, add ginger, chillies and onions, cover and cook over a medium heat for 10-15 minutes or until onions are golden. Stir in tomatoes and cook over a low heat for 10-15 minutes or until tomatoes are soft. Stir lentil mixture and 4 cups/1 litre/1 3/4 pt water into tomato mixture and bring to the boil.

3   Heat ghee or butter in a frying pan, add cumin seeds, fennel seeds, mustard seeds, fenugreek seeds, black onion seeds, ginger, bay leaves and garlic paste (if using) and cook for 2 minutes. Stir spice mixture into boiling lentil mixture, cover and cook for 2 minutes longer.

To microwave: Place lentils, ginger, turmeric, salt to taste and 2 cups/500 mL/ 16 fl oz boiling water in a large microwave-safe dish and cook on HIGH (100%) for 8 minutes, then on MEDIUM (70%) for 10 minutes or until lentils are cooked. Make sauce and prepare spice mixture as described above. Stir sauce and spice mixture into boiling lentil mixture and cook for 2 minutes longer.

Serves 6

RICE WITH PEAS AND SPICES

2 tablespoons vegetable oil
2 teaspoons finely chopped fresh ginger
1 fresh red or green chilli,
finely chopped
$^1/_4$ teaspoon cumin seeds
$^1/_4$ teaspoon black mustard seeds
3-4 fresh or dried curry leaves
salt
1 tablespoon chopped fresh basil
1 tablespoon chopped fresh mint
1 tablespoon chopped fresh coriander
90 g/3 oz fresh peas, half-cooked
2 cups/440 g/14 oz rice
4 cups/1 litre/1$^3/_4$ pt boiling water
10-12 strands saffron soaked in a little
warm water (optional)

Serves 6

1   Heat oil in a large heavy-based saucepan, add ginger, chilli, cumin seeds, mustard seeds, curry leaves and salt to taste and cook, stirring, for 1 minute.

2   Stir in basil, mint, coriander, peas, rice, water and saffron mixture (if using), cover and bring to the boil. Reduce heat to low and cook for 15 minutes or until rice is cooked.

To microwave: Place oil, ginger, chilli, cumin seeds, mustard seeds, curry leaves and salt to taste in a microwave-safe dish. Cover and cook on HIGH (100%) for 3 minutes. Add basil, mint, coriander, peas, rice, water and saffron mixture (if using) and cook on HIGH (100%) for 7-8 minutes, then on LOW (30%) for 15 minutes. Fluff up with a fork before serving.

Rice with Peas and Spices

Joan Bowers

INDIAN BREADS

Bhutoras

Pau

Pooris

Chapatis

Parathas

*Clockwise from right: Chapati,
Pau, Paratha, Poori, Bhutora*

BHUTORAS

3 teaspoons sugar
1¼ cups/155 g/5 oz flour
¾ teaspoon bicarbonate of soda
1 cup/200 g/6½ oz natural yogurt
3 cups/470 g/15 oz sifted
wholemeal flour
salt
1½ tablespoons melted ghee or butter
¾ cup/185 mL/6 fl oz lukewarm water
vegetable oil for deep-frying

1 Place sugar, flour, bicarbonate of soda and yogurt in a bowl and mix to combine. Cover with plastic food wrap and set aside to ferment overnight.

2 About 3 hours before you intend to cook Bhutoras, place wholemeal flour, salt to taste, ghee or butter and water in a bowl. Stir in yogurt mixture and mix to form a dough. Turn dough onto a lightly floured surface and knead well for 15 minutes, adding flour, if necessary, to make a firm smooth dough.

3 Divide dough into 16 equal portions and roll out each portion to form a thin round. Heat oil in a wok until very hot but not smoking. Slip 1 bhutora into oil at an angle so that it is submerged in oil. Using a large flat round slotted spoon gently hold bhutora under oil for 2-3 seconds or until you feel it rise. Rapidly spoon oil over bhutora and as soon as it puffs up and blisters, turn it over and continue spooning oil over until bhutora puffs and blisters again. Remove and drain on absorbent kitchen paper.

Makes 16

When sifting wholemeal flour for Bhutoras, Parathas, and Chapatis use a fine sieve and discard the husks.
If the recipe states sifted flour it should be measured after sifting. If it states flour or flour, sifted, it should be measured before sifting.

PAU

8 round bread rolls
butter

1 Cut bread rolls in half and spread each cut side with butter.

2 Melt a little butter in a large frying pan and cook bread rolls on both sides until golden. Serve immediately.

Serves 8

POORIS

2¹/₂ cups/375 g/12 oz wholemeal flour
1 cup/125 g/4 oz flour
salt
1 cup/250 mL/8 fl oz water
vegetable oil for dough and deep-frying

1   Sift wholemeal flour, flour and salt to taste together into a bowl. Discard husks. Stir in 1 teaspoon oil and enough water to form a soft dough. Turn dough onto a lightly floured surface and knead until smooth. Place dough in a bowl, cover and set aside for 30 minutes.

Makes 16

2   Knead dough again for 5 minutes and divide into 16 equal portions. Roll each portion into a ball. Flatten each ball and roll out to form a thin 6 cm/2¹/₂ in round.

3   Heat oil in a wok until very hot, but not smoking. Slip 1 poori into oil at an angle so that poori is submerged in oil. Using a large flat round slotted spoon gently hold poori under oil for 2-3 seconds or until you feel it rise. Rapidly spoon oil over poori and as soon as it puffs up and blisters, turn it over and continue spooning oil over for 3-4 seconds longer. Remove and drain on absorbent kitchen paper.

If the oil is not hot enough the poori will not rise and if it is too hot the poori will burn and, again, not rise. Cooking Pooris takes a little practice but is well worth the effort.

CHAPATIS

2 cups/315 g/10 oz wholemeal flour
¹/₂ cup/60 g/2 oz flour
salt
vegetable oil
1 cup/250 mL/8 fl oz lukewarm water

1   Sift wholemeal flour, ¹/₄ cup/30 g/1 oz flour and salt to taste together into a large bowl. Discard husks. Mix in 1 tablespoon oil and enough water to form a firm dough. Turn dough onto a lightly floured surface and knead for 10 minutes or until dough is smooth. Place dough in a bowl, cover and set aside for 1 hour.

2   Knead dough again then divide into 12 equal portions. Roll each portion into a ball. Flatten each ball, sprinkle with a little of the remaining flour and roll out until quite thin to make an oval shape. Rub a little oil onto each oval.

3   Place thumb and middle finger on opposite sides of each oval and squeeze together to form 2 circles. Fold circles

together so oiled sides are in the centre, dust with a little more flour and roll out again.

4   Heat a little oil in a frying pan over a medium heat and cook Chapatis one at a time for 2-3 minutes each side. Drain on absorbent kitchen paper.

Makes 12

Cooked Chapatis will keep in an airtight container for up to 3 days.

PARATHAS

2 cups/315 g/10 oz sifted
wholemeal flour
1¹/₂ cups/185 g/6 oz flour
2 tablespoons vegetable oil
³/₄ teaspoon salt
water
vegetable oil for dough

1   Place wholemeal flour, flour, oil and salt in a bowl and mix to combine. Stir in enough water to form a soft dough.

2   Turn dough onto a lightly floured surface and knead for 5-7 minutes or until dough is smooth and soft and no longer sticky. Place dough in a lightly oiled bowl, cover and set aside for 30 minutes.

3   Knead dough for 5 minutes longer. Divide dough into 16 portions and roll each portion into a ball. Flatten each ball and dust with a little flour, then roll out to a 15 cm/6 in round, dusting with flour as necessary. Brush with oil, fold in half and brush with oil again. Fold to form a triangle, dust with flour and roll out to a 15 cm/6 in triangle. Brush with oil.

The cooked Parathas should be golden with dark brown patches. Wrap cooked Parathas in aluminium foil and place in the oven at 120°C/250°F/Gas ¹/₂ to keep warm, or reheat when required.

4   Heat a large cast-iron frying pan over a medium heat. Add a little oil, then cook 1 paratha at a time for 1 minute or until air bubbles start to form. Turn and cook other side until golden.

Herb Parathas: At the end of step 1, add to the soft dough 2 tablespoons chopped fresh coriander, 1 tablespoon chopped fresh mint, 1 tablespoon chopped fresh dill, 1 tablespoon snipped fresh chives and 3 fresh green chillies, very finely chopped.

Makes 16

STARTERS

EGGPLANT ENTREE

500 g/1 lb eggplant (aubergine)
2 cloves garlic
1 fresh red or green chilli
2 teaspoons chopped fresh ginger
4 tablespoons chopped fresh coriander
$^1/_4$ cup/60 mL/2 fl oz lemon juice
3-4 slices white bread
1 cup/250 g/8 oz sour cream
salt
freshly ground black pepper
mini toast to serve

1   Hold eggplant (aubergine) over a medium flame or place under a preheated grill and cook, turning frequently, until eggplant (aubergine) is soft and skin is loose and can be easily removed. Set eggplant (aubergine) aside to cool and when cool enough to handle remove skin and chop flesh.

2   Place eggplant (aubergine), garlic, chilli, ginger, 3 tablespoons coriander, lemon juice, bread, sour cream, and salt and black pepper to taste in a food processor or blender and process to make a smooth paste.

3   To serve, pile eggplant (aubergine) mixture in centre of a serving platter, sprinkle with remaining coriander and surround with mini toast.

Serves 6

From right: Eggplant Entrée, Spicy Stuffed Mushrooms, Spicy Chicken

SPICY CHICKEN

4 boneless chicken breast fillets, cut
into large cubes
2 tablespoons cream (double)
3 cloves garlic, finely chopped
2 fresh red or green chillies,
finely chopped
2 teaspoons finely chopped fresh ginger
1 bunch fresh basil, leaves
removed and chopped
salt
$1^1/_2$ teaspoons ground coriander
$1^1/_2$ teaspoons ground cumin
1 teaspoon garam masala
$^1/_4$ teaspoon ground cardamom
$^1/_4$ teaspoon ground cinnamon
1 teaspoon mango powder
1 teaspoon ground turmeric
pinch ground cloves
pinch ground nutmeg
$^1/_4$ cup/60 mL/2 fl oz lemon juice

1   Place chicken, cream, garlic, chillies,
ginger, basil and salt to taste in a bowl
and mix to combine. Combine coriander,
cumin, garam masala, cardamom,
cinnamon, mango powder, turmeric,
cloves and nutmeg and stir into chicken
mixture. Cover and marinate in
refrigerator for 8-10 hours.

2   Thread chicken cubes onto four
skewers and cook, turning frequently,
under a preheated grill or on a preheated
barbecue for 8-10 minutes or until
chicken is cooked. Sprinkle with lemon
juice and serve immediately.

Serves 4

Spicy Chicken is delicious
served with a salad such as
Cabbage Salad (page 46)
or Fresh Green Vegetable
Salad (page 32).

Pewter Platter Made Where

SPICY STUFFED MUSHROOMS

Oven temperature
150°C, 300°F, Gas 2

8 large mushrooms
15 g/^{1}/2 oz butter
1 tablespoon vegetable oil
2 onions, chopped
2 teaspoons finely chopped fresh ginger
2 fresh red or green chillies,
finely chopped
1 teaspoon cumin seeds
3 tomatoes, chopped
1 teaspoon ground cumin
^{1}/4 teaspoon ground turmeric
^{1}/2 teaspoon mango powder
1 teaspoon ground coriander
1 bunch fresh coriander, leaves
removed and chopped
salt

Alternatively, the mushrooms
can be cooked in the
microwave on HIGH (100%)
for 5-7 minutes or until
cooked.

Serves 4

1   Remove stalks from mushrooms.
Chop stalks finely and set aside.

2   Melt butter in a large frying pan, add
mushroom caps and cook for 1-2 minutes
each side. Remove mushrooms from pan
and place in a shallow ovenproof dish.

3   Heat oil in pan, then add onions,
ginger, chillies and cumin seeds and cook,
stirring frequently, for 5-7 minutes or
until onion is soft and pinkish in colour.

4   Add chopped mushroom stalks and
tomatoes and cook for 10 minutes or until
tomatoes are soft and pulpy. Stir in
ground cumin, turmeric, mango powder,
ground coriander, half the fresh coriander
and salt to taste and mix to combine. Fill
each cooked mushroom with a little of
the tomato mixture, sprinkle with
remaining coriander and bake for 20
minutes.

FISH PATTIES

500 g/1 lb boneless white fish fillets
2 teaspoons finely chopped fresh ginger
2 fresh red or green chillies,
finely chopped
1 bunch fresh coriander, leaves
removed and chopped
1 teaspoon cumin seeds
1 teaspoon lemon juice
pinch garam masala
salt
2 eggs, lightly beaten
dried breadcrumbs
vegetable oil for shallow-frying

The batter will keep in the
refrigerator in an airtight
container for up to 4 days.

1   Steam or microwave fish until just
cooked. Flake fish and place in a bowl.

2   Add ginger, chillies, coriander, cumin
seeds, lemon juice, garam masala and salt
to taste to fish and mash to combine.

3   Take spoonfuls of fish mixture and roll
into balls. Dip each fish ball in egg
mixture than roll in breadcrumbs to coat.

4   Heat 2.5 cm/1 in oil in a large frying
pan and shallow-fry patties for 3-4
minutes each side or until golden. Drain
on absorbent kitchen paper and serve
immediately.

Makes 20

MEAT PATTIES

2 potatoes, diced
2 cardamom pods
1 large onion, chopped
250 g/8 oz veal or lamb mince
2-3 fresh red or green chillies,
finely chopped
1 teaspoon cumin seeds
$^1/_2$ bunch fresh coriander, leaves
removed and chopped
1 teaspoon fresh ginger, finely chopped
3 cloves garlic, finely chopped
1 egg, lightly beaten
salt
vegetable oil for shallow-frying

Fish Patties,
Meat Patties   **Makes 20**

1   Place potatoes and cardamom pods in a saucepan, add just enough water to cover and bring to the boil. Reduce heat and simmer for 10 minutes or until potatoes are cooked.

2   Add onion and mince and cook for 5 minutes longer. Drain off excess liquid, remove cardamom pods and set potato and meat mixture aside to cool for 15 minutes. Add chillies, cumin seeds, coriander, ginger, garlic, egg and salt to taste to potato and meat mixture and mash to combine. Form mixture into patties.

3   Heat 2.5 cm/1 in oil in a large frying pan and shallow-fry patties for 3-4 minutes each side or until golden. Drain on absorbent kitchen paper and serve immediately.

The pattie mixture will keep in an airtight container in the refrigerator for 2-3 days.

Elephant Joan Bowers Plates and Mat Bay Tree Kitchen Shop

LENTIL DUMPLINGS

Lentil dumplings are delicious served with whipped yogurt sprinkled with salt, paprika and mango powder.

The lentil paste will keep in an airtight container in the refrigerator for 2-3 days.

1 cup/200 g/6¹/2 oz mung dhal (small yellow lentils), cleaned
1 teaspoon yellow mustard seeds
1 teaspoon cumin seeds
¹/4 teaspoon ground turmeric
¹/4 teaspoon mango powder
pinch bicarbonate of soda
salt
2 tomatoes, finely chopped
1 bunch coriander, leaves removed and finely chopped
2 teaspoons finely chopped fresh ginger
2 fresh red or green chillies, finely chopped
vegetable oil for deep-frying

Makes 20

1   Place lentils in a bowl, cover with water and set aside to soak for 3 hours. Drain and place lentils, mustard seeds, cumin seeds, turmeric, mango powder, bicarbonate of soda and salt to taste in a food processor or blender and process to make a coarse paste.

2   Transfer lentil paste to a bowl. Add tomatoes, coriander, ginger and chillies and mix to combine.

3   Take spoonfuls of mixture and roll into small balls. Heat oil in a large saucepan until a cube of bread dropped in browns in 50 seconds. Cook lentil dumplings a few at a time for 3-5 minutes or until golden and cooked through.

POTATO PATTIES

1 kg/2 lb potatoes
12 slices white bread
water
2 teaspoons lemon juice
2 fresh red or green chillies, very finely chopped
1 bunch fresh coriander, leaves removed and very finely chopped
vegetable oil
salt
dried breadcrumbs

Makes 20

1   Boil or microwave potatoes until tender. Drain, place in a bowl and mash.

2   Place bread slices in a bowl, pour over enough water to cover and set aside to soak for 5 minutes. Squeeze as much water as possible out of the bread.

3   Add bread, lemon juice, chillies, coriander, a dash of oil and salt to taste to mashed potatoes and mix well to form a dough. Rub the middle of the palms of your hands with a little oil, then take a small amount of dough and roll it into a ball. Flatten ball slightly to form a round pattie. Coat pattie with breadcrumbs. Repeat with remaining dough.

4   Heat 2.5 cm/1 in oil in a frying pan and cook patties a few at a time for 2-3 minutes each side or until golden. Drain on absorbent kitchen paper and serve immediately.

*Lentil Dumplings: cooking dumplings;
(in bowls) mung dhal and lentil dumpling mixture*

DESSERTS

*Indians feel that sweets are a must after every meal.
Traditionally, Indian desserts are very sweet. In these recipes
the sugar has been reduced by at least half to make the desserts
more appealing to Western palates.*

Indian Fruit Salad with Rabri

Sweet Rice
Tayri

Yogurt Almond Ice Cream
Shrikand

Semolina Pudding
Sooji Halwa

Wholemeal Halva
Seera

Rose-flavoured Sweet
Gulab Jamboo

*Indian Fruit Salad with Rabri,
Sweet Rice*

Plates and glass Studio Hans

Indian Fruit Salad with Rabri

1 apple, cored, peeled and diced
1 pear, cored, peeled and diced
2 peaches, stoned, peeled and diced
1 small bunch grapes
1 mandarin, segmented, pips removed and flesh diced
2 slices pawpaw, peeled and diced
1 mango, peeled and diced

RABRI
8 cups/2 litres/3^1/$_2$ pt milk
1^1/$_2$ cups/375 g/12 oz sugar
^{1}/$_4$ teaspoon vanilla essence
1 teaspoon ground cardamom
100 g/3^1/$_2$ oz pistachio nuts, sliced

1   Steam or microwave apple, pear and peaches, separately, until tender.

2   To make Rabri, place milk in a heavy-based saucepan and bring to the boil, reduce heat to low and simmer, stirring occasionally, for 1^1/$_2$ hours or until reduced by half.

3   Stir in sugar, vanilla essence, cardamom and pistachio nuts and cook, stirring occasionally, until sugar dissolves. Serve Rabri either warm or chilled.

4   To serve, arrange apple, pear, peaches, grapes, mandarin, pawpaw and mango in a serving dish and spoon over Rabri.

Serves 4

Indians eat only small quantities of desserts, but cook up large quantities and then keep them. The desserts in this chapter will keep in the refrigerator for up to a week.

Sweet Rice

15 g/^{1}/$_2$ oz ghee
1 cinnamon stick
1^1/$_2$ cups/330 g/10^1/$_2$ oz long grain or basmati rice
2 tablespoons sultanas
5 strands saffron soaked in ^{1}/$_4$ cup/ 60 mL/2 fl oz warm water
silver leaf (optional)
2 tablespoons sliced pistachio nuts

SUGAR SYRUP
4 cups/1 litre/1^3/$_4$ pt water
1 cup/250 g/8 oz sugar
1 teaspoon rosewater
^{1}/$_2$ teaspoon ground nutmeg
pinch ground cardamom
pinch ground cinnamon

1   To make syrup, place water, sugar, rosewater, nutmeg, cardamom and cinnamon in a large saucepan and cook over a medium heat, stirring occasionally, for 10 minutes or until sugar dissolves.

2   Heat ghee in a heavy-based saucepan. Add cinnamon stick and cook, stirring, for 30 seconds. Remove cinnamon stick and discard. Add rice to pan and cook, stirring constantly, for 3-5 minutes. Add sultanas and saffron mixture and cook for 2 minutes. Stir in sugar syrup and cook for 15 minutes or until rice is tender.

3   Transfer rice to a serving platter, cover with silver leaf (if using) and sprinkle with pistachio nuts. Serve warm with cream or ice cream.

Serves 6

YOGURT ALMOND ICE CREAM

500 g/1 lb natural yogurt
500 g/1 lb caster sugar
45 g/1^1/$_2$ oz ground almonds
1 teaspoon ground cardamom
pinch ground cinnamon
pinch ground nutmeg
pinch yellow food-colouring powder
2-3 drops almond essence
2 tablespoons sliced pistachio nuts
2 tablespoons sultanas
1 tablespoon sliced unblanched almonds

1   Place yogurt in a colander lined with cheesecloth and set over a bowl. Allow to drain for 2-3 hours. Turn yogurt into a clean bowl, add sugar, ground almonds, cardamom, cinnamon, nutmeg, food-colouring powder and almond essence and whip until soft and fluffy.

2   Stir in pistachio nuts, sultanas and almonds. Spoon mixture into a freezerproof container and freeze for 30 minutes or until required.

Serves 6

This ice cream will keep almost indefinitely in the freezer.

SEMOLINA PUDDING

30 g/1 oz ghee
2 cups/400 g/12^1/$_2$ oz fine semolina
1 tablespoon sultanas
1 tablespoon unsalted pistachio nuts
^{1}/$_2$ cup/125 mL/4 fl oz milk

SUGAR SYRUP
2 cups/500 mL/16 fl oz water
2 cups/500 g/1 lb sugar
1 tablespoon cardamom seeds
pinch yellow food-colouring powder

1   To make syrup, place water, sugar, cardamom seeds and food-colouring powder in a large saucepan and bring to the boil over a medium heat. Strain syrup, set aside and keep warm.

2   Melt ghee in heavy-based saucepan, stir in semolina and cook over a low heat, stirring constantly, for 20-30 minutes or until semolina changes colour slightly. Take care not to burn the semolina.

3   Stir sultanas and pistachio nuts into semolina mixture and cook for 3 minutes. Stir in Sugar Syrup and milk and cook over a low heat, stirring constantly, for 5 minutes or until mixture thickens.

To microwave: Melt ghee in a large microwave-safe container on HIGH (100%) for 60 seconds. Stir in semolina, cover and cook on HIGH (100%) for 2 minutes, then on MEDIUM-HIGH (90%) for 4 minutes, stirring after 2 minutes. Stir in sultanas, nuts, milk and Sugar Syrup and cook on MEDIUM (70%) for 4 minutes. Mix well.

Semolina Pudding is delicious served with cream or ice cream.

Serves 6

Yogurt Almond Ice Cream,
Semolina Pudding

WHOLEMEAL HALVA

1 cup/250 g/8 oz sugar
2 cups/500 mL/16 fl oz water
30 g/1 oz ghee
2 cups/315 g/10 oz sifted
wholemeal flour
pinch ground cardamom
2 tablespoons chopped pistachio nuts
2 tablespoons sultanas
silver leaf (optional)

1   Place sugar and water in a large saucepan and bring to the boil over a medium heat. Reduce heat and simmer for 5 minutes.

2   Melt ghee in a heavy-based saucepan, add flour and cook, stirring constantly, until flour starts to leave the sides of the pan. Stir in sugar syrup and cardamom and cook, stirring, for 2-3 minutes longer.

3   Remove pan from heat, stir in pistachio nuts and sultanas. Spoon halva into a serving dish and decorate with silver leaf (if using). Serve warm.

Serves 6

Wholemeal Halva

Glass Bay Tree

Rose-flavoured Sweet

ROSE-FLAVOURED SWEET

GULABS
1 cup/75 g/2^1/$_2$ oz skim milk powder
^{1}/$_3$ cup/45 g/1^1/$_2$ oz self-raising flour
15 g/^{1}/$_2$ oz ghee or unsalted butter
100 mL/3^1/$_2$ fl oz cream (double)
vegetable oil for deep-frying

SUGAR SYRUP
7 cups/1.6 litres/3 pt water
3 cups/750 g/1^1/$_2$ lb sugar
^{1}/$_2$ teaspoon ground cardamom
1 teaspoon rose essence or
2 teaspoons rosewater

1   To make syrup, place water, sugar, cardamom and rose essence or rosewater in a large saucepan, cover and bring to a slow boil over a low heat.

2   To make Gulabs, place milk powder, flour and ghee or butter in a food processor and process to combine. With machine running, add enough cream to form a moist dough. Roll dough into 2 cm/^{3}/$_4$ in balls.

3   Heat oil in a wok or large saucepan until a ball dropped into the oil sizzles slowly. Reduce heat, add remaining Gulabs and cook, stirring gently, until Gulabs rise to the surface. Using a flat, slotted spoon, roll spoon over top of Gulabs, turning them constantly until they are dark golden brown in colour.

4   Increase heat under syrup. Remove Gulabs from oil and add to boiling syrup. Reduce heat and cook for 2-3 minutes or until Gulabs expand and become soft. Remove pan from heat and set aside to cool. Serve Gulabs warm or at room temperature with ice cream or cream if desired.

Makes approximately 20 Gulabs

When cooking the Gulabs in the oil they must be rolled constantly and cooked quickly to prevent them from drying out and cracking. When cooking Gulabs in the syrup take care not to leave them in the syrup for too long or they will become too soft and will break.

DRINKS

Lemon Drink
Limbu Pani

Sweet Yogurt Drink
Mithi Lassi

Spicy Tea
Chai

Mango Yogurt Drink
Aam Lassi

Spicy Coffee
Indian Coffee

Thadhal

LEMON DRINK

juice 4 lemons
6 cups/1.5 litres/2¹/₂ pt water
¹/₂ teaspoon salt
4 tablespoons sugar
16 fresh mint leaves
4 slices lemon

1   Place lemon juice, water, salt and
sugar in a food processor or blender and
process for 1 minute or until sugar
dissolves.

2   Pour into a large jug, stir in mint
leaves and lemon slices, cover and
refrigerate for at least 30 minutes before
using.

Serves 6

*From right: Thadhal, Lemon Drink,
Spicy Coffee, Spicy Tea, Sweet
Yogurt Drink, Mango Yogurt Drink*

Glasses Bay Tree Kitchen Shop Cup and Saucer Made Where Silver Dish Joan Bowers

SWEET YOGURT DRINK

3 cups/600 g/20 oz natural yogurt
2 cups/500 mL/16 fl oz water
$^{1}/_{4}$ teaspoon ground cardamom
2 teaspoons rosewater
2 tablespoons caster sugar

Place yogurt, water, cardamom, rosewater and sugar in a food processor or blender and process to combine. Serve immediately.

Serves 4

SPICY TEA

3 cups/750 mL/1$^{1}/_{4}$ pt milk
1$^{1}/_{2}$ cups/375 mL/12 fl oz water
3 cardamom pods, slit
6 strands lemon grass or 2 teaspoons
finely grated lemon rind
2 teaspoons chopped fresh ginger
2-4 teaspoons sugar (optional)
1 teaspoon fennel seeds (optional)
1 teaspoon ground cinnamon (optional)
4 teaspoons tea leaves

Place milk, water, cardamom, lemon grass or lemon rind, ginger and sugar, fennel seeds and cinnamon (if using) in a saucepan and bring to the boil. Stir in tea leaves and cook over a low heat for 2-3 minutes. Cover and set aside to draw for 2-3 minutes. Strain into cups and serve immediately.

Serves 4

MANGO YOGURT DRINK

3 cups/600 g/20 oz natural yogurt
2 cups/500 mL/16 fl oz water
pinch ground cardamom
1 teaspoon rosewater
2 tablespoons caster sugar
1 fresh mango, diced

Place yogurt, water, cardamom, rosewater, sugar and mango in a food processor or blender and process to combine. Serve immediately.

Serves 4

SPICY COFFEE

3 cups/750 mL/1^1/4 pt milk
1^1/2 cups/375 mL/12 fl oz water
3 cardamom pods, slit
pinch ground nutmeg
^{1}/2 cinnamon stick
3 teaspoons sugar (optional)
2 tablespoons coarsely ground
coffee beans

Place milk, water, cardamom, nutmeg, cinnamon and sugar (if using) in a saucepan and bring to the boil. Stir in coffee, reduce heat to low and simmer for 2-3 minutes. Strain into cups and serve immediately.

Serves 4

THADHAL

4 cups/1 litre/1^3/4 pt milk
2 tablespoons pistachio nuts,
coarsely ground
2 tablespoons walnuts, coarsely ground
2 tablespoons cashews, coarsely ground
2 tablespoons almonds, coarsely ground
1 teaspoon vanilla essence
^{1}/4 teaspoon ground cardamom
^{1}/4 teaspoon rosewater
2 teaspoons caster sugar
^{1}/4 teaspoon rose-flavoured syrup
(optional)

Place milk, pistachio nuts, walnuts, cashews, almonds, vanilla essence, cardamom, rosewater, sugar and rose-flavoured syrup (if using) in a food processor or blender and process until well blended. Transfer mixture to a large jug, cover and chill well before serving.

Serves 4

To make rose-flavoured syrup, simply add a little rose essence or rosewater to a sugar syrup.

'The drinks in this section make a refreshing accompaniment to Indian food.'

INGREDIENTS

The magic of Indian cooking lies in the myriad of herbs and spices used. Every dish derives its unique taste from the different blending of herbs and spices.

There is a myth that Indian food is 'curry' – meat in a sloppy gravy – and is only good when it's hot and your mouth is crying for iced water! This concept of curry originated with the British, who ruled India for more than 200 years. They invented a mixture of spices – hot ground cayenne pepper, ground cinnamon, nutmeg, cloves, turmeric, ground cumin and ground coriander. This powder (curry powder) is never used by Indian cooks! Firstly, some of these spices are just not used together and, secondly, every dish tastes the same when you use curry powder. Indian cooks make their own mixtures of various spices for different dishes. To use just one combination of

spices is to forget that India has many, many, different regional cuisines, each with its own distinctive flavour.

The secret of any dish is the mixture (masala) of spices used and the length of the cooking time. Spices and herbs should never be overcooked or they will lose their flavour. Avoiding overcooking also means you can prepare food up to 2 days ahead and still not lose the fragrance and flavour.

For almost every dish I cook, there are eight ingredients I like to use: these are cumin seeds, ground coriander, mango powder, ground cumin, ground turmeric, salt, fresh ginger and fresh chillies.

THE SPICES

Bay leaves *(Tej Patha)*: This spicy, aromatic but mellow-tasting leaf is used in sauces and rice dishes (pullaos).

Black onion seeds *(Kalaunji)*: These have no connection with onions but are so called because they resemble onion seeds. They are mainly used in rice dishes and with green, leafy vegetables in stir-fried dishes. Black onion seeds have a strong bitter-sweet flavour.

Black peppercorns *(Kali mirch)*: A pungent condiment that is used whole in chutneys. Ground black peppercorns are used mainly in yogurt and salad dishes.

Black salt *(Kali namak)*: This is a hard block of sulphurous rock which is spicy and extremely pungent. It should not be tasted or used by itself! (Keep it away from children.) Use black salt only when mixed with other ground, dry spices in chutneys,

sauces and toppings. It can be purchased as a piece of rock which you can grind then keep in an airtight container; or it can be bought ready-ground.

Note: If black salt is omitted when called for in a recipe the dish will lack the distinctive flavour.

Cardamom *(Elaichi)*: Cardamom provides an aroma which many Indian dishes require. It also helps digestion and is one of the spices used in garam masala. There are three types of cardamom. Black pods are used mainly in rich Moglai dishes. They are also used in a spice bag for rice and have a slightly spicy taste. Green pods are used mainly in pickles and desserts. The seeds are also used in syrups. The pods and seeds have a slightly sweet taste. Ground cardamom is used as one of the ground spices in main meals, yogurt drinks and Indian tea (*chai*).

Cayenne pepper (Degi mirch): This is the ground powder of a red pepper originating from Kashmir. It is very hot and should be used in minute quantities in meat dishes and sweet chutneys. It can be used in place of the whole peppers.

Cinnamon (Dalchini): This has a sweet spicy flavour. It is used whole in pullaos, desserts and chutneys. Ground, it is one of the spices used in garam masala and is used in meat and chicken dishes and some desserts.

Coriander (Dhania): The seeds are used whole to flavour lentils and in some vegetable dishes. Ground coriander has a distinctive taste and is one of the eight 'must' spices in my cooking! But don't get carried away and add too much to food or it will be overpowering.

Chillies (Mirch): These come in several varieties, but the following are four of the most commonly used:
Fresh red chillies: These come in a variety of shapes and sizes. As a general rule, the smaller, narrower and darker the chilli, the greater its pungency.
Fresh green chillies: These are 5-10 cm (2-4 in) long and are rich in vitamins. They give a distinctive hot taste to food and will keep in an airtight container for 7-10 days.
Ground chillies: Mainly used with fried vegetables as a topping. Add ground chillies according to your own taste.
Dried chillies: Used in spice bags for pullaos and pickles.

Cloves (Laung): These have a pungent taste and aroma. Ground cloves are one of the main spices used in garam masala. Whole cloves are used in rich Indian dishes and chutneys. Ground cloves are used in tiny amounts in some desserts.

Cumin (Jeera): This spice is used both as whole seeds and as the ground spice. The whole black seeds have a sweet herbal taste and are used in northern and Moglai dishes and in biriyanis. The white or green seeds are used whole or ground and are one of the most important spices in the eight spices that I use. I feel my food is incomplete without this subtle, gentle flavour. It is used in appetisers, snacks, batters and yogurts. Ground cumin is another of the spices in

garam masala. It has a fragrant and warm aroma.

Curry leaves (Curry pata): These are available both fresh and dried from Indian food shops. They have an aromatic flavour and are used in certain vegetable dishes and as a topping for yogurt.

Fennel (Saunf): The seeds are similar to white cumin seeds and are used mainly in pickles, drinks and rice dishes. Fennel seeds are also used to aid digestion after eating. Ground fennel is used in meat, chicken and fish dishes and gives a tangy minty bite.

Fenugreek (Methi): The seeds, mainly used in lentil, and some vegetable, dishes have a bitter taste. Ground fenugreek is used mainly in meat, chicken and fish dishes. Fenugreek leaves can be bought fresh or dried and are used as a flavouring for vegetables or as a herb. They have a bitter-sweet taste.

Garlic (Lasan): This is the root of a plant and is a very important ingredient in nonvegetarian dishes, some lentil dishes and chutneys.

Garam masala: The name means 'mixed spice' and it consists of cinnamon, cloves, cardamom, cumin, nutmeg, black peppercorns and coriander ground together. It can be bought ready-mixed in the spice section of most supermarkets.

Ginger (Adrak): Used both fresh and ground, ginger is the aromatic root of a tropical plant. Fresh ginger is a must in all Indian cooking and it has to be peeled before use. Ground ginger is used mainly as a topping with other dry spices for salads, fried vegetables, sweet dishes and in marinades.

Hing (Asafoetida): This is a hard block of resin which is used as an aid to digestion and to prevent flatulence. It is used mostly when cooking lentils and pulses. In India the block would be heated in a hot oven for 5 minutes and then ground to a fine powder in a mortar and pestle. In the West it can be purchased already ground. It is used in minute quantities.

Kewra essence: This is a flavouring obtained from a flower and is used in desserts.

Mace *(Savitri)*: This spice is used ground in chutneys.

Mango powder *(Amchur)*: This is a brownish powder made from sun-dried green mangoes and is one of the eight 'must' spices in my cooking. It has a sour taste and gives a unique flavour which is loved all over India.

Mustard seeds *(Rai)*: These come in three colours, black, brown and yellow. Black mustard seeds are used mainly in vegetarian sauces, to flavour yogurt and in vegetable dishes. Brown mustard seeds are more difficult to find but are better than black in chutneys and toppings. Yellow mustard seeds are used in lentil and vegetable dishes with a tomato base.

Nutmeg *(Jaiphal)*: This spice is used in small quantities to give a subtle flavour to meat and rice dishes. It is also used in sweets and puddings.

Paprika: This spice is used mainly as a topping for salads.

Poppy seeds *(Khus-Khus)*: These are used as a thickening agent in desserts and give a special texture to food.

Saffron *(Kesar)*: This is a very expensive spice which comes from either Kashmir or Spain. It has an aromatic flavour and is used to colour desserts and rice dishes.

Sesame seeds *(Til)*: These are mainly used in chutneys, pickles and some sweets.

Turmeric *(Huldi)*: One of my eight 'must' spices, turmeric is an aromatic, pungent root. It is used ground to colour and flavour meat and vegetable dishes. Take care when using turmeric as it can stain.

THE HERBS

Basil *(Tulsi)*: Indians worship the basil plant. I like to use the leaves for yogurt and rice dishes and in sauces. Basil has a sweet, sharp taste.

Chives: Used in salads and with other herbs in vegetable dishes, chives have a mild onion flavour.

Coriander *(Kutmir)*: Indian cooks use only the leaves of fresh coriander. When chopped they have an aromatic flavour and are used as a garnish, in chutneys and for sauces.

Dill *(Sowa)*: Used in vegetable dishes, salads and some rice dishes, dill has a clean delicate flavour.

Mint *(Phudina)*: This herb is used in salads and chutneys, and is mixed with other herbs in vegetable dishes.

OTHER INGREDIENTS

Caster sugar *(Cheeni)*: This is used in salads as well as some meat and vegetable dishes.

Coconut *(Nariyal)*: Used as flakes in lentil (dhal) dishes or grated in salads and some vegetable dishes.

Lemon juice *(Limbu Ras)*: Used in many recipes to give a tangy taste.

Mustard oil *(Rai-ka-Tel)*: This is used in small quantities in pickles.

Palm sugar *(Gur)*: Used in chutneys and lentil (dhal) dishes.

Sesame seed oil *(Til-ka-Tel)*: Used in salads to give a nutty flavour.

Silver leaf *(Vark)*: This is used as a garnish on pullaos and desserts. It is available from some Indian food shops and art supplies shops.

Tamarind *(Emli)*: Available as pieces or as a concentrate, tamarind is used in lentil (dhal) dishes and chutneys.

The more unusual spices, herbs and other ingredients should be available from Indian and Asian food shops.

INDEX